LEARN HIGHER PAYING SKILLS

STEVE CHURCHILL

Thanks David, for believing the book
was worth a revision.

CONTENTS

1 RESKILLING YOURSELF

Is this book for you? This book is for you if you're dissatisfied with your work, career, or income and you feel responsible to do something to improve them.

"After all is said and done, more is said than done."

Look at this book as a **workbook**. Each chapter contains important things for you to **do**. Those things will help you improve your career, income, and business if you have or want one. This book is divided into three sections:

Section 1: You'll learn more about the benefits of *reskilling* yourself. You'll determine *why* you should keep learning new skills, how it will improve your life, and what consequences you might face if you don't keep learning.

Section 2: Different people learn differently. You'll discover *how* you learn best. You'll identify your own learning preferences and develop custom strategies for learning new skills.

Section 3: After reading about **why** and **how** you can learn new skills, you'll get an overview of *what* to learn: the essential abilities needed to improve your career and income. You'll see that the things we cover in this section are applicable to any career path or business.

What This WORKbook Will Do for You

Getting better work and income requires persistent effort on your part to learn and apply the principles in each chapter. It will take time to master them.

Job Hunters and Career Movers: As you work through the chapters and exercises, you'll develop the ability to learn new skills more quickly. You'll create a "toolbox" for adapting to evolving job markets and technologies. While others worry about *job security*, you'll feel confident and secure in your own *marketability*.

Business Owners and Aspiring Entrepreneurs: If you're an entrepreneur or thinking about starting your own business, the ability to teach yourself will ensure you remain competitive and successful. One exciting aspect of having your own business, in addition to making more money, is the opportunity to learn so much about running a company. The faster you learn, the faster you'll succeed.

You don't have to work through the chapters in order. You can read and take notes on the sections you feel are most relevant to you and your situation. If you're reading an electronic version of this, there are instructions on taking notes in eBooks within the section on *Active Learning*.

Be sure to **complete the *Challenge* activities** in each chapter. They're designed to help you practice the skills and apply the information. These exercises will help you retain your new knowledge.

2 WHAT IS HIGHER PAYING?

Do you feel "higher paying" is only about a bigger paycheck, or does it include things like job satisfaction, better working hours, more friendly coworkers, and things like that? Let's explore what it is you're looking for in your work and income. Knowing what you really want is a first step in defining your path to get there.

After spending a lot of time and money in school, no one wanted to offer me a high paying job. I felt devastated! You might say, "You see, college isn't worth it!" I'm not going to say that. I believe that **depending on what your goals are**, a college education may or may not serve your purposes. My problem was that I didn't understand how the business world really operated–what it is that companies truly value. Fortunately, I spoke with someone who helped me change my perspective.

A friend referred me to a director of training at a large company. He said he didn't have any open positions, but he'd look at my resume. Later, when I called him to follow up, he opened my email, took a glance at my resume, and said, "Oh! You're just right out of college! You don't know anything!" You see, I put my college degrees right there at the top of my resume. But how could he look at my academic credentials and say something like that? Did he have any idea how much work my education required and how much debt I incurred to get it?

When I didn't respond, I think he felt bad, so he clarified what he meant. He explained that it was a great thing I had those degrees. He believed many businesses don't care what or how many degrees someone has, they simply want to know how you'll make or save them money. He suggested that I put my work experience first on the resume and call out my key accomplishments.

Now, this book isn't primarily about job hunting or resumes but the skills we cover should help improve those for you. I mentioned this experience because the reality-check I got helped me change my attitude. As you go through this book, keep in mind that:

> **What you really like doing and what people are willing to pay well for may be two entirely different things.**

Your Job is Your Fault

A few years ago, a disgruntled corporate mailroom worker complained about how he hated his job and had to find better work. In my mind, I thought of an imaginary email I could send him. Then I realized the message applied more to me than it did to him:

Mailroom Guy,

You know, about a year ago you told me how much you hated your job working in the mailroom. You said, "I have to get outta here. This job's killing me!" I asked what kind of work you wanted to do instead, and you didn't have any idea. I thought you'd only be around for a few more weeks considering how upset you were.

But 12 months later, you're still here stuffing mailboxes and pushing that blasted cart around the offices! Have you tried to learn a new skill? Have you enrolled in any classes? What do you do with your free time? If you want better work and income, then you've got to get qualified and go get it.

Do you know that these executives walking around here make anywhere from $200,000-$500,000 a year?!? Is it because they work any *harder than you? I don't think so. You bust your butt around here. Those guys **work smart more than they work hard.** If we don't like our jobs or feel our compensation isn't fair, let's do something about it.*

If we spend 30 minutes a day learning something new, that would add up to about 180 hours in a year that we could use to develop some expertise. We could become investing wizards in that amount of time. Or, we might learn how to start our own businesses. We could master Internet marketing and e-commerce on the road to a fortune!

Think of it! Believe you can do it. Take all that hatred you've got for your job and redirect it into channels that will get you better work. Stop complaining and start complying with what it takes to get a more rewarding career.

And you'd better not still be here in a year. I'll come back to check!

The truth is, I also spent too much time in jobs that didn't pay well and offered no real opportunities for advancement. Eventually, I woke up and realized, **"You must take charge of your own learning and development for more rewarding work!"**

Your Financial Well Being

Are you tired of waiting for something to happen that suddenly gets you a more enjoyable job? How long have you hoped for enough money to pay your bills? What if you don't have the time, money, or desire to go back to school? You're probably tired of:

- Waiting for the economy to get better.

- Waiting for your boss to appreciate the quantity and quality of work you do.

- Hoping your business will suddenly improve.

- Waiting to get a raise or promotion you deserve.

- Searching through hundreds of job listings on the Internet, applying to dozens of them, and never hearing back from recruiters even though you feel well-qualified for the positions.

Our financial and career frustration might come from trying to play a new game by old rules. Global, local, and personal economic catastrophes will continue to make businesses, employers, and customers fearful of taking risks.

Businesses delay investment for new projects because they're uncertain about the payoff. Companies hesitate to create new positions or offer raises and promotions. This isn't only a problem for the unemployed, it's also a problem for the people who *are* employed and have much heavier workloads.

Unfortunately, some employers now pass over unemployed people altogether when they try to fill open jobs. One news article reported that companies and recruiters are wary of hiring someone that another company saw fit to let go. With high unemployment, some job seekers misrepresent their work experience in desperate attempts to get hired.

Small business owners worry when their revenues decrease. Many of them find that simply spending more money for more employees or marketing ends up being a waste of money.

If we're to succeed financially and professionally, we've got to learn the new rules of this new game. And we need to learn quickly!

As we've observed, the economy is ruthless. It doesn't care about your career, your goals, or your efforts to provide for yourself and your family. The economy doesn't care that your job–your source of pride and income–suddenly vanishes and reappears in another country. The economy doesn't care if your career is suddenly vaporized by a new technology or invention. The trend of "creative destruction" is the new, permanent way the game is played.

Creative Destruction: "Innovation causes failure, but that failure, in turn, creates more innovation."

You'd like to have a rewarding job that's challenging. You want work that makes use of your unique talents and hard-earned skills. You may dream of running your own successful business. Sure, you'd like to become wealthy by doing that work, but just having enough to pay the bills and buy a few nice things would be great for now.

Higher paying–in terms of money–varies depending on how much you're earning now. If you're unemployed, higher paying means more money (and more self-respect) than you're receiving from unemployment checks. If you've been stuck in the same job making $30K per year, higher paying may mean $5K or $50K more per year and opportunities for advancement. If you own a business, it may mean doubling or tripling your sales.

The U.S. Department of Labor and the U.S. Census have helpful information on the average salaries by profession/position. You can find recent salary information by searching the internet for *department of labor salary statistics* and *census data earnings*. A few other online resources for salary and income information are available at: *Indeed.com/salary* and *Payscale.com*.

Using these tools (it's best to research more than one site), determine where you're at in terms of compensation and where you want to be in the future. Identify those positions and industries that offer the type of pay you seek.

Another important note is that self-employed people or small business owners aren't always listed in these types of reports because their businesses, industries, and job titles are so different. The average yearly income for sole proprietors and small business owners is almost $100K! (According to *SimplyHired.com*) As you consider what you need to do to get better work and income, remember that it may not simply mean getting a new job. Your path may lead to self-employment.

How can you escape the trap of poor employment and low income? How can you learn higher paying skills without spending years and thousands of dollars on more formal education? Consider this:

"You are what you learn. It's easy to feel trapped in your own life. Circumstances can sometimes feel as if they form a jail around you. But there's almost nothing you can't learn your way out of. If you don't like who you are, you have the option of learning until you become someone else. Life is like a jail with an unlocked, heavy door. You're free the minute you realize the door will open if you simply lean into it."
-Scott Adams, Dilbert.com (Emphasis added)

Challenge: Determine What You Want

The most effective learning is driven by a specific purpose. You purchased this book because you want better work and income, so take some time before you work through the lessons to define what "better work and income" means to you. Answer these questions and share your thoughts with a friend or family member:

- **Answer this**: What does "better work and income" mean to you?

- You may be unemployed and simply want a steady job with a fair paycheck. Are you willing to accept some entry-level work as a step in that direction? Why or why not?

- You may have a high paying job already, but want "better work" that offers more time to take care of your health and family. How can you do this and stay afloat financially?

- You may be stuck in a dead-end job and plan on starting your own business. What type of work would you do, and how much money do you hope to make?

Challenge: Sustain Commitment & Motivation

This isn't the first personal or professional development book you've bought. Did you finish the last one? Did it produce the results you wanted? We often feel excited and determined when we set a goal or start a new program, then those feelings fade. Answer these questions:

- How will you sustain your motivation to finish this program?

- What will happen if you don't learn the skills necessary to get better work and income?

Education Versus Academics

People have pointed out that *education* opens the door to economic opportunity. I believe that fully. But **education and academics aren't necessarily the same thing**. Sometimes you must complete formal, expensive higher education to learn what's needed for your career goals. Many times, you do not.

When I've asked accomplished professionals and businesspeople how much of what they needed to know to succeed was something they learned in school, the almost unanimous response was "very little." Most of what they learned to succeed were things they learned on-the-job, through hard experience, or from mentors.

I don't want to discourage anyone from putting time and money into formal education and degrees if that's your path. I want to encourage anyone who doesn't have the time or money to go that route by showing there are other ways to get that *education* and open doors of economic opportunity for you. What are they? Read on!

Summary:

- An unpredictable economy and job market are forcing you to take charge of your own learning and development to get better work and income.

- "Learning how to learn" is the most important skill you can develop for income security and career success.

- You need to define what "better work and income" mean to you and how you'll sustain your motivation to get them.

3 UPSKILLING CASE STUDIES

The next few pages contain some real-life examples of people who found themselves in unfavorable work or income situations. As you read through these, see if you can relate to any of them and what the examples have in common.

One young man, a few years out of high school, loved working with computers but didn't want to do any more formal education. He got an entry-level job working in packaging and deliveries. Realizing there wasn't any long-term opportunity in that, he bought several books on computer programming and started learning more on his own. He installed a basic network at the company he worked for. When another business owner heard about what this young man could do, he hired him for a much higher wage. This self-taught computer programmer has worked with that same company now for more than 20 years and has done very well financially. He enjoys an amazing amount of flexibility to choose when and where he works.

A woman spent several years focusing on raising her children instead of fulltime employment. She decided to get back into the workforce. Facing the dilemma of needing experience to get work but not being able to get work without experience, she decided to get certified as a life coach. She enrolled in a reputable life coaching program, earned her certification, and did a lot of free coaching work to build her credibility. She's now earning decent money doing something she loves.

Another stay-at-home mom wanted to do something to earn money while her kids were in school. She needed the flexibility to shuttle them around and attend their activities, so she started her own cleaning business. She never ran a business before and didn't have the time to take any formal schooling. She bought an armful of entrepreneurial business books, committed her two successful business-owner brothers to mentor her, and started asking people if they needed cleaning help. Within a few years she had a multi-million dollar commercial and residential cleaning business with dozens of employees.

One middle-aged man spent a few decades working in the defense industry and decided he wanted out of that corporate world. He loved to teach but knew that teaching college as an untenured professor, he wouldn't make enough money to support his large family. Acting in faith that things would work out, he enrolled in a masters then a doctorate program while maintaining his fulltime job. He earned his Ph.D. He secured a position teaching college and got hired as an account manager for a large software company's academic clients. The two roles complimented each other, paid him good money with the combined salaries, and let him do something he felt was more worthwhile.

A woman who had three children and had been married for about a decade faced a terrible situation when her husband—the sole income earner— suddenly divorced her. Financially, she couldn't wait for any alimony or child support payments. They proved to be inadequate when they came anyway. With no real employment history to speak of and no formal training, she took a job working in a medical office as a filing clerk. She enrolled in an online degree program and earned her bachelor's degree a few years later. She eventually got better employment, earned the necessary income, and received the healthcare benefits her family needed.

A machinist once worked all week while the business owners took their friends on a hunting trip. He did everything from turning the lights on to writing up and mailing the invoices to customers. The total amount of work he billed that week was over $10K but his paycheck for that week was only $1K. He'd had enough after that. Within a few weeks he quit that job and opened his own machining and repair service. He already acquired much of the tooling he needed. He talked (and listened) to several people like accountants, marketers, and other business owners to learn what he needed to do to stay in business. Now, almost twenty years later, he's been able to hire several people and do well financially even during economic downturns.

A nearly-retired consultant experienced a large drop off in business in 2008. He didn't feel he was in a financial position to entirely leave the workforce. Companies weren't spending as much as they used to for his type of consulting services. He decided to take much of his written training material and turn it into online video courses. He didn't let all the technology requirements intimidate him: he took courses, joined online teaching groups, studied the platforms and technology, then learned to do basic video recording and production. He's succeeded in building a large online offering of courses and makes several thousands of dollars each month in recurring income from them. He continues to learn marketing and production techniques to keep his courses relevant and competitive.

A newlywed woman took a job at the corporate headquarters of a large national company. She earned significantly less than others in her same role because she didn't have a college degree. With a child on the way, she knew she'd have even less time in the future to get more education. So, she finished her bachelor's (bachelorette's?) degree. She also earned multiple certifications in the human resources and training industry. Within a few years, she got another job at a new company and quickly earned a promotion to an executive position.

An industrial supply salesman spent several years building up business accounts for his employers, only to see his commissions reduced and sales quotas increased. He shared a story that helped increase his motivation to start his own business:

"A man stopped by to talk to his neighbor who was sitting out on the front porch. As the two chatted, the neighbor's dog, lying on the wood steps, occasionally moaned and groaned. After it did this a few times, the man asked his neighbor, 'Is your dog OK? Why does he keep making those noises?'

The neighbor said, "It's 'cuz he's lying on a nail sticking up through the floor.'

'Well, why doesn't he just get up and lay somewhere else then?"

The man's neighbor said, "I guess it's cuz **it doesn't hurt enough yet!***"*

This disenchanted salesman decided it hurt enough already, learned what he had to do to start a business, and successfully built a thriving business. Think of your own situation. **Does it hurt enough yet?**

From your perspective, what do all these examples have in common? First, these are real people and their stories are real. Their circumstances are all similar in that they wanted better jobs or needed more income. **Each of them recognized their own responsibility to improve their situations. Each of them saw learning as the gateway to a better career or life.**

They each took slightly different paths to learn what they needed to know. Some took a more formal route with college classes and certifications. Others bought stacks of books to study. Some of them relied on mentors and on-the-job training. Any of these can work successfully. The next section of this book will help you identify learning strategies that might work best for you.

Potential Consequences

Before moving on, let's consider a few more examples. However, these are cases where the people *would not* or *could not* update their skills to get better work and income.

One middle-aged man documented and trained employees on computer systems for most of his career. He received certifications in these systems and his experience made a great career for him. *Until it didn't*. Still too far from being able to retire and unwilling to adapt to the new systems, his employer eliminated his position. Unable to find new employment in the specialties that had sustained his career for so long, he had to take entry-level work in retail sales to support himself.

A recent college graduate completed a degree in marketing and felt passionate about working in the marketing or advertising field. She refused to apply for unrelated jobs and felt overqualified for any sales positions (which can often lead to other work in marketing). She held out hope for over two years that someone would hire her for a marketing role. She believed she was qualified for that type of work based on her degree alone—with no real-world work experience. When her refusal to consider any other job, and the fact that she stayed home or shopped all day began to jeopardize her marriage, she finally relented and got hired for a different type of role.

A father with a large family teaches high school. He likes the work and the students he teaches, but the salary doesn't cover the increasing costs of providing for his family. He works a second job in the evenings and on weekends, but the pay from that barely compensates for the shortfall of his main salary. He'd find a new career if he had the time. He doesn't have any money available to pay for more education or training. He feels like he's a slave to his own immediate needs and doesn't see any way out of his circumstances

What do these last three examples have in common? Each of these people are unable or unwilling to learn and adapt to improve their unfavorable circumstances. In a few of the cases, they weren't willing to accept their *response-ability* to change those circumstances. All three of their stories should scare us because any one of them could be our story.

The information in this book is meant to avoid these types of situations or to get us out of those circumstances if that's where we're at now. The next section is going to show **how** to best avoid career and income pitfalls by learning new, more marketable skills.

Challenge: What it Means for You

Answer these:

- What do the examples in this chapter have in common with your situation?

- Did the people who succeeded have any superpowers or miraculous intervention to help improve their situations? What should that communicate to you?

- What will happen in your own life and career if you fail or refuse or forget to take responsibility for your learning and development?

SECTION 2: HOW TO LEARN NEW, HIGHER PAYING SKILLS

To summarize Section 1, you've defined **why** you need to accept responsibility for your own learning to get better work and income. You have a clearer idea of what it is you want and need in a paycheck and in the type of work you do. You've renewed your commitment to find a better career. The examples of people who have and haven't made these changes provided you with even more motivation.

This next section of the book presents some basic information about learning theory. You'll learn how to apply those ideas to your own career development path. You'll see that everyone learns differently. You'll also see that formal schooling isn't always right for everyone. Many people learn very effectively in places other than a classroom.

You'll learn about the differences between *active* and *passive* learning. This section also contains some strategies for making your learning engaging and how to concentrate better. When you complete the challenges, you'll have a solid, workable plan for how you're going to learn new career skills.

4 HOW YOU CAN LEARN BETTER AND FASTER

Consider this story based on a real person's experience.

David forced himself to study a few thick books on computer programming languages. He had an opportunity to get promoted at work if he could earn a few specific *Microsoft* certifications. He bought the certification study guides and spent his evenings after work reading through them. A month later, when he thought he was ready for the certification test, he paid the expensive testing fee, took the test, and failed miserably!

After all that studying, David didn't understand why he performed so poorly on the test. He didn't give up. He decided to change his approach to learning what he needed to know. Instead of forcing himself to spend several hours in the late evening reading the study guides, he got up a little earlier in the morning and read for thirty minutes before work. He read for another thirty minutes during his lunch break and studied for an hour in the evenings. He also listened to quiet music while he studied and found an Internet forum where he could get advice from others who had already passed the certification.

The next time David took the test, he did very well and earned the certification. I don't know if he received the promotion he wanted yet, but **the way he adapted his learning practices** seemed to make all the difference for passing the test. Did you pick up on these important points about what he changed?

- At first, David forced himself to study for several hours late in the evening after he'd already spent a full day at work. The next time around, he divided up his learning time into shorter sessions throughout the day.

- He made his learning experience more enjoyable by listening to music while he studied.

- He also got help from others who had already learned the skills he was trying to master.

As I create various training programs for employees in large organizations, I need to develop training that accommodates many different learning styles and preferences. When it comes to skill development, some people want to see it demonstrated. Others want it explained to them. Another group of people want to dive in and try it themselves. Good training incorporates all three approaches.

Now, what about your learning preferences? How can you improve your learning habits to master higher paying skills? Do you know how you learn best? Understanding your own learning preferences will accelerate your skill development and help you get better work and income more quickly.

Learning Channels

Learning theory classifies the process of acquiring new knowledge into three main channels:

- **Hearing**: Learning from verbal communication or explanations of new concepts and information.

- **Seeing**: Learning through visual communication or demonstrations that convey concepts or processes.

- **Doing**: This is "hands-on" learning or practice; it's experimentation and activity to gather new information and understanding.

Chances are that **you prefer a combination of all these channels**. Or, your preferred channel may change depending on what you're trying to learn. For example, if you're studying history or business principles, then reading or hearing an explanation might be enough. You may need to see a diagram or video to understand how a process or machine works. If you need to know how to repair a computer, the best path to mastery might be by grabbing the tools, reviewing the instructions, and working through it yourself.

So, how should you approach learning new skills when any one (or a combination) of these methods might work best for you? You'll cover all your bases by following a simple process that incorporates all three learning preferences.

An Effective Learning Process

In the training industry we accommodate a wide range of learning preferences by following a simple process. It's effective because most people learn best with a combination of the methods we just discussed. Follow this sequence:

1. **Hear It**: Have someone who's knowledgeable on the subject *explain* it to you. Ask questions for clarification. Write down what they *say* in your own words.

2. **See It**: Find someone who can *show* you how to effectively apply that skill. Look for a demonstration, diagram, or video on the Internet. *Watch* other experts to see how they work.

3. **Try It**: *Practice* using the new skill. Find someone who will observe and give you feedback. Use instructions or notes as you *work through it*.

4. **Apply It**: Put the new skill or knowledge to *work in the real world*. The more often you apply what you've learned to a real situation, the more likely you are to retain that information or ability.

You can take this approach to learning new skills on your own. You'll master these new abilities more quickly. Remember that repetition is necessary to master new knowledge and skills. *Repetition is necessary to master new knowledge and skills.*

Challenge: Determine Your Learning Preferences

Think of a skill you learned well in the past. How did you learn it effectively? Did you read a book? Did someone else coach you? Identifying what's worked well for your learning and development in the past can help you recreate those same conditions for learning new skills in the future.

Ways You Can Learn

Reading a book is only one way to learn something new. Here are some other ways to learn. Some of them are obvious to you, some may not be:

- Have an expert explain a process
- Role-play with someone
- Draw a diagram to represent a process
- Watch an instructional video
- Take a college course
- Teach or share new information with someone
- Take notes and keep a study journal
- Start a blog on the subject
- Find a coach or tutor
- Listen to an audio program
- Volunteer, apprentice, or intern to learn more
- Observe an expert or professional at work
- Perform trials or experiments to see what does or doesn't work

- Search the Internet for information (more about how to do this better in a later chapter)
- What other ways can you think of to learn new skills?

Challenge: Your "To-Learn" List
Identify the skills you'd like to learn. List some of the methods or resources you can use to learn those new skills.

- A skill you would like to learn:

- Ways you can learn it:

- Another skill you would like to learn:

- Ways you can learn it:

Create Your Own Learning Plans
Now that you've considered options for learning new skills, you need to create a plan to accomplish your skill development. Start by writing down a specific, measurable goal and the target date to accomplish it. You also need to define a purpose or incentive for your learning goal. Let's look at important elements of your learning plan.

Determine What's in It for You
Theories about how adults learn best indicate they need to know exactly how they'll benefit from learning a new skill. Will I make more money? Get promoted? Run a

business more effectively? Experience less stress through the workweek? While learning just for the sake of learning is enjoyable, it's a luxury we can't afford when we're worried about financial survival or employment security.

If you want to accelerate your own learning and career development, keep reminding yourself of your motivation for learning the new skill. Include it as part of your learning plan. For example:

- "I'm learning management skills so I can get promoted, make more money, and start advancing my career."

- "I'm learning how to market my services so I can start my own business and quit my 9-to-5 office job."

- "I'm learning negotiation and selling skills so I can close more sales and generate more revenue for my company, and more commissions for myself!"

- "I need to learn this computer programming skill so I can make more money and get out of debt!"

- "I will learn the principles of finance and investing so I can retire in five years!"

After that, write down the most effective options available to master that new knowledge or skill based on your learning preferences. Share your learning plan with someone who will hold you accountable for it. Post the paper with your plan on the wall, or take a photo of it to use as a background image on your computer or mobile device. This will keep your learning plan on your mind. Some important points to remember about creating a learning plan include:

- The more specific you are about what you want to learn (why, how, and when to learn it), the more likely you'll be to accomplish this goal.

- How you'll learn the new information or skill should include a variety of methods that incorporate multiple learning channels.

- Learning with someone else will accelerate your progress. Find another person who wants to develop the same skill as you and create a shared learning plan.

- You need to devise some test or benchmark for yourself that determines whether you've truly mastered the skill or not. For example, if someone's goal was to learn web design, her "test" might be to see if she can create an entire website without referring to books or notes.

A Sample Learning Plan:

- **Goal**: Learn HTML 5 and be able to create an entire mobile-friendly website using this web design standard.

- **Why**: The design tools and programming languages I know will become obsolete really fast. If I want to remain competitive and earn good income as a web/interactive designer, I've got to master HTML 5.

- **When**: By the end of this year.

- **How**: Purchase a book on HTML 5, work through one chapter each week, and complete all the exercises. Create a website to experiment with. Connect with someone in my design networking group who knows HTML 5.

Challenge: Create Your Own Learning Plan

Identify a new skill you should develop to improve your career. Complete each section of the plan for how you'll master this skill. Create learning plans for other skills you want to develop. Remember to include these elements:

- Goal (what you want to learn):

- Why (the payoff for learning it):

- When you'll learn it (deadline):

- How you'll learn it (using some of the strategies from earlier, or others you've thought of):

Summary:

- You'll learn a new skill most effectively by hearing or reading an explanation, viewing a demonstration, and then applying and practicing the skill.

- You have many different options for learning new skills and information. You don't necessarily have to spend a lot of time and money in college courses to master the skills that pay well.

- Once you've selected which skills to learn to improve your career or business, you should write out a simple and specific learning plan. The learning plan should include details about what you want to learn, why you want to learn it, when, and how you plan on learning it.

5 MAKE YOUR LEARNING ACTIVE LEARNING

How are you feeling at this point about your ability to take control of your circumstances and learning for better work and income?

In one of my jobs as an instructional designer at a large satellite TV company, I rewrote most of the training program for new installation technicians. I understood that every new technician had a different preference for learning. But for the most part, the technicians who came through the program wanted to learn the skills by trying and repeating them—they were *active, hands-on* learners.

Instead of rewriting a thick instructional manual on how to install satellite TV systems, I simply created a series of checklists. Trainees were given options to learn the skills on their own, refer to process documents, or they could be coached through each process by their assigned field trainers. Many of them used all three options.

This modified approach to the new-hire training program got the employees up-to-speed much more quickly. It saved the company money because trainers and technicians spent a lot less time in the classroom and spent more time getting work done. The revised program transformed the training program from passive learning into active learning. They learned their new skills quicker and applied them much more consistently.

Do you want to spend a lot of time developing a new skill and end up forgetting it? No! You want to make your learning efforts as effective as possible. You want to get the maximum return for your investment. You want to ensure your goals to develop higher paying skills truly bring better work and income. You can acquire new skills and knowledge faster **by transforming your passive learning habits into active learning habits**.

Active learning couples the exposure to new information with some type of activity that increases understanding and retention. You should get into the habit of immediately applying what you've learned. This chapter contains a few ways you can transform your learning approach to become more effective and profitable.

Why You Should Avoid Passive Learning

Passive learning is simply trying to "absorb" new knowledge and information without expending much effort. It's sitting, listening to a lecture or program without taking notes, without asking questions, or even really thinking about the information. Passive learning may even include reading a book without underlining, cross-referencing or note taking. Passive learners often hope they'll understand and retain that information just by absorption. Is that realistic? Unfortunately, you'll waste a lot of your time and effort if you try to learn things passively.

What is Active Learning?

To repeat what you read a moment ago, **active learning couples the exposure to new information with some process or activity that increases your understanding and retention**. It may include stopping to ask the presenter for more details or clarification on a subject. Active learning could involve taking notes, creating outlines, or drawing diagrams while you're being taught. If you're that type of **visual** learner, check out the books and videos on *Sketchnoting*. Active learning may also include role playing a skill or practicing a procedure until it becomes a habit. You'll master the information or ability more quickly, retain it longer, and do it correctly. Let's look at a few active learning strategies.

How to Read and Mark Up a Book

Some editions of Dale Carnegie's book, *How to Win Friends and Influence People*, contain instructions about how readers can get the most from their study. Among other things, he suggests that readers go through each chapter twice and underline important ideas. You should develop your own system for reading and marking up books or other reading material. Developing your own note taking system will not only make your reading much more productive, it will create a useful tool for reviewing information.

Your own marking system should have a ranking to it. For example, rate the importance of concepts on a level of 1-4 and have a different symbol or mark to call it out. Here's an example for marking up reading material:

- Level 1 – Interesting ideas: Write parenthesis around the (interesting idea)

- Level 2 – Important concept: Put brackets around the [important idea]

- Level 3 – Critical concept: <u>Underline the critical concept or information</u>

- Level 4 – Super-Critical: Draw a box around the super-critical information

Developing a personalized system for summarizing and "digesting" reading material will help accelerate your professional development. You may also **read out loud** for better understanding and memory of what you read. People around you might learn something as well!

Distill the information you acquire from reading. Don't simply underline and highlight passages in the text. When you read an important passage or paragraph, write a short summary of the main point out in the margin of the book.

If there's not enough room in the margins of the book to write your summary notes, you can write your comments into a notebook or computer document. **These summaries need to be in your own words!**

Some people feel books should be revered and never written in. I feel they're tools for learning and you can use them however you want (at least the books you own). I've even torn pages out of books and pinned them to my walls because the information was that important. So, when it comes to reading, listening to audiobooks, or watching instructional videos, develop your own marking and summarizing system to increase your understanding and retention of what you read, see, and hear.

Why You Should Take Notes

Taking notes does a lot more than create a document to refer to when you need to review information. In fact, when you actively create good notes, you don't need to refer to them very often to recall information! That may not seem to make sense; let me explain.

The process of summarizing and taking notes cements new knowledge more fully into your brain. It converts the information that sits in your temporary, short-term memory into your more permanent, long-term memory. The more engaging your own note taking process is, the less dependent you'll be on those notes. It seems contradictory, but it's true.

Actively taking notes on what you read or hear doesn't necessarily mean writing everything down. You can draw a diagram that attempts to establish relationships between the concepts a speaker or author presents. While reading an article or viewing a presentation, you can create an outline that summarizes and establishes a hierarchy or timeline for that information. Again, look up the term *sketchnoting* to learn about ways to make notetaking a more visual, engaging process. An acquaintance of mine published his notes from a college program in a book called *The Visual MBA* that provides great examples.

Digital Note Taking

You may be reading the electronic version of this book instead of a printed copy. You may prefer reading on a computer, tablet, or phone. If that's the case, you can take digital notes to ensure you actively learn and retain the information. Research the functionality of your device to see how you can insert notes into the document itself (the *Kindle* has this ability). There are also several desktop and mobile apps available for quickly capturing information and adding your own notes to it. Look at *Evernote, Microsoft OneNote, Google Keep, Notability*, and *Apple Notes* to see if any of these tools will work for you.

You can also copy and paste text into a word document. Be sure to include source links and page numbers, as well as a summary of the information in your own words for any notes you copy.

Challenge: Back to the Beginning

If you haven't done it already, go back and create your own notes for the previous chapters in this book. Write a short summary (in your own words) of each section's main points. Don't skip this exercise! When you develop a system and habit of taking notes for what you read or hear, you'll retain and apply much more of what you learn.

Apply Your New Knowledge and Skills

Most of the active learning techniques discussed so far have to do with understanding and retaining new information—how you can transform *information* into *knowledge*. How do you experience active learning when it comes to something you need to *do*? Do it as soon as possible after seeing a demonstration or hearing an explanation and then practice it a few times. If an instructor demonstrates how to do something, don't be afraid to ask, "Can I try that myself?"

If the new skill is something like how to communicate more effectively, or how to give someone feedback, then role play it with someone else. Role playing is "acting out or performing the part of a person or character, as a technique in training." (Oxford dictionary) Make a goal to try it in your next conversation. Remember that **a lesson that's not applied is a lesson that's lost!**

Learning to Teach to Learn

One of the most effective ways to master new skills and information is by **teaching them to someone else**. Share what you learn. Knowing that you'll do this in advance motivates you to listen, watch, or read more intently. As you try to explain the new task or concept to someone else, it helps you understand and remember it better yourself. Teaching what you've learned to someone else will help you identify gaps in your own understanding. You might discover that you need to go back and review something you've studied. Ultimately, sharing what you've learned will build your self-confidence in your new skills and knowledge.

Challenge: Teach Someone Else

Think of some people you know who might appreciate the information you've covered so far in this course. Or, choose a topic you know you need to learn more about.

Answer these questions:

- Who do I want to share my new knowledge with?

- What I will teach them?

Challenge: Activate Your Learning

This lesson discussed a few ideas about how you can use active learning to increase your understanding and retention. Create a list of other ways to make your learning more active:

-

-

-

-

-

-

Summary

- You'll master new knowledge and skills more quickly with active learning.

- Active learning requires something more than just reading a book or listening to an instructor.

- Taking notes and writing your own summaries of what you learn will help you embed new information into your memory.

- Remember that a lesson that's not applied is a lesson that's lost!

- Teaching someone else what you're trying to learn will help you master it much more rapidly and increase your confidence in your new knowledge.

6 IMPROVE YOUR ATTENTION SPAN AND CONCENTRATION

Consider the following story, based on a real person's experience, and ask yourself how being able to focus and concentrate better will help you achieve your career goals.

Maria recently launched her own medical supply business. While she knows a lot about the healthcare industry from her career as a registered nurse, she discovered that she didn't know enough about marketing and selling to effectively build her business. She never learned well by sitting down at a desk studying for long periods, so she decided to simply spend five minutes each day reading something new about selling. She writes down a new quote about sales strategies on a notecard every morning, and tries to apply that concept to her client interactions that day.

She keeps the notecards in a box and occasionally reviews them to refresh her memory. By following this simple habit for a few months, Maria has increased her confidence and selling skills. Her business is doing extremely well. She's even considering an offer from a larger medical supply company to purchase her business.

Your chances for learning higher paying skills depends on your ability to pay attention and concentrate. As children, we were often told to, "Pay attention!" Yet, we were not taught *how* to pay attention. This chapter discusses the challenges you face when trying to pay attention. We'll look at strategies to improve your attention span and concentration.

What Is My Attention Span?

Your attention span is the length of time you can focus on something before you become bored or overloaded with information. That amount of time varies from person to person and depends on the type of activity. You're likely to maintain a longer attention span while doing an active, hands-on project than listening to a presentation. You're also more likely to pay attention and concentrate longer while being *entertained* than when you're being *taught*. Great presenters and teachers successfully blur the line between entertainment and teaching. Consider these definitions:

- **Paying Attention**: The act or state of applying the mind to an object or thought; a selective narrowing or focus of consciousness or receptivity.

- **Attention Span**: The length of time an individual is able to concentrate or remain interested.

Your Attention Has Been Hijacked!

Cases of Attention Deficit Hyperactivity Disorder (ADHD) continue to rise proportionate to increased TV, Internet, video game, and portable media use. Marketers compete viciously to get your attention. It takes louder noises, brighter lights, and more extreme headlines to get you interested. These tricks leave your mind numb and unable to focus on your work, creativity, and studies. As you realize that there's a war going on for control of your mind–and as you fight back–you can increase your attention span and strengthen your ability to focus.

Copywriters, reporters, and filmmakers design most forms of media to get and keep your attention. They essentially hijack your thoughts. TV programs leave you in suspense right before a commercial break. Novels draw you in with a "hook" at the end of each chapter to keep you reading. Newspapers, websites, and magazines project sensational or controversial headlines and curious images to get people to click them.

The children's program *Sesame Street* launched in the late 1960s and targeted preschoolers with an educational and entertaining TV show. One person involved with the show wrote: *"Our work was research into education, child psychology, and how people of all ages learn. It concluded that music, color, movement, and involvement were essential factors in enhancing the learning process."* (*Trainers in Motion*, by Jim Vidakovich)

People at Children's Television Workshop (CTW) conducted experimental trials of certain programs with a young audience. They'd have other things going on offstage–deliberately–observing which programs riveted the children's attention despite the offstage distractions. Programs with lots of color, movement and music **captivated** their audiences.

What began as a seemingly worthwhile cause soon mutated under the influence of marketers and media outlets. They've learned to manipulate our minds! They take our eyes and ears hostage with well-researched combinations of sound and images.

How many colors, bright lights, and fascinating sounds do you observe in video games? They're so consuming that they make a parent or spouse's voice inaudible to the gamer. How do movies keep our attention for two and three hours at a stretch? Study cinematography or simply count how many times a camera angle changes within a few minutes.

Too many outside influences enslave our abilities to concentrate. We're left numb and jaded, held back from focusing on learning activities which will improve our lives.

Challenge: What Things "Steal" Your Attention?

- Make a list of things that divert your attention from more productive activities:

- Then answer this: How can you prevent these things from taking control of your ability to concentrate?

How to Get Your Attention Back

Unplug! How many of our daily activities depend on electricity or batteries? When we expose ourselves to so much electronic media that's designed to take our attention away, we won't have any "pay attention power" left when we need it most.

Practice concentrating despite distractions. When baseball players warm up their swings before walking to home plate, the weights they place on their bats require them to exert additional effort. When they step up to home plate and swing at the pitched ball (with the weights removed), they use more force and generate faster bat speed. Studying or reading with some ambient noise like music or traffic can help you redouble your concentration and focus on the subject much more. With practice, you can learn to block out even more disruptive distractions.

Build up mental endurance. There's a type of conditioning used in the athletic world called interval training. This consists of regular, timed periods of high exertion followed by systematic intervals of less intense activity. Overall stamina and performance improve more quickly (and with less injury) when compared to long periods of intense workout. You can apply this principle to mental development. Partition your study and learning time with regular breaks to let your mind rest and recover.

Have you ever heard someone say, "My brain hurts?" Learning to build up mental endurance with bursts of concentration followed by periods of *thoughtless* recovery will make your learning time more effective. This habit will also promote a better attitude and generate more enthusiasm for the whole learning experience.

Too often, you may think of concentration as a long, headache-causing session of staring at a book or computer screen placed a few inches from your face. The more time that you spend forcing yourself to do this, the less effective each passing minute will be. Those attempts to concentrate produce a diminishing return.

Some learning theories say the mind processes information in **chunks**. The ideal number of these chunks that the mind can handle in each session is about seven. You'll find that your endurance for how long you can concentrate will grow over time. With discipline and practice, your ability to concentrate will strengthen like an exercised muscle.

You'll improve your concentration by focusing on learning for shorter sessions more frequently. Instead of setting aside a head-splitting two-to-three-hour block of time for learning a new skill, schedule several smaller pockets of 15-30 minutes throughout the day. You'll understand and remember information better by taking this approach.

Learn what you love. One of the most effective ways to increase your attention span is to spend your time learning things you're passionate about. *Wanting* to learn something will help you pay attention and concentrate much longer than when you feel *required* to learn something.

Challenge: Conduct Your Own Experiment
Take a subject that you're learning about (perhaps this book itself) and try studying it for a two-to-three-hour block. Then over the next few days (not on the same day as the long session) study it for about thirty minutes each day. Answer the following questions:

- How much information do you recall from the long study session compared to the shorter sessions?

- Which was more enjoyable?

- How should this affect your learning habits?

Find Your Effective Learning Flow
There's a psychological concept called flow. It's defined as a mental state where you're fully immersed, energized, focused, and involved in an activity. See the book titled *Flow,* by Mihaly Csikszentmihalyi. You may have to experiment a little, but you can achieve this mental and emotional state while learning new skills. Consider these ideas as you try to establish your own effective learning flow:

- You need to have a specific goal, a clear idea of what you want to master or achieve. Review the information about creating your own learning plans in the earlier chapter.

- You need to have a clear incentive for learning the new skill or information like more money, a better job, or more sales, and constantly remind yourself of that payoff.

- You need to have a process for how you'll acquire that skill or knowledge.

- You need to have the right resources available to learn what you need to know like the right books, access to the Internet, a coach or mentor, tools, etc.

- You need to create an environment that's favorable to your learning style. It needs to minimize distractions. It needs to be comfortable enough to learn effectively, but not too comfortable that you fall asleep.

As you identify the environment and conditions that work best for your own learning flow, you'll find that you can pay attention and concentrate for longer periods of time.

Challenge: Your Effective Learning Environment

- At what time of day do you learn best?

- Do you learn best indoors or outdoors?

- Are you sitting or standing?

- Do you learn best at home, in a library, in a workshop, or some other place?

- Write down some thoughts about your preferred learning environment–where and when you experience the best learning flow.

Summary:

- Many things in your environment attempt to hijack your attention. You need to learn how to control what you pay attention to if you want to learn higher paying skills.

- You'll learn best when you concentrate for smaller amounts of time throughout the day instead of one longer session.

- You need to identify and create the type of environment where you can get into an effective learning flow. *Flow* is that state where you are fully engaged in your learning activity.

7 ASK EFFECTIVE QUESTIONS

An old proverb says, "Those who ask questions are fools for a minute; those who do not, remain fools forever." A massively important part of your learning and career development will be asking the right questions.

Have you ever had a child ask you to explain something? Did the child continue to ask, "why" after every detail you attempted to provide?

"Why's it raining, dad?"
"Because a storm came in last night, son."
"Why's there a storm, Dad?"
"Because a lot of clouds got together."
"How do the clouds get there, Dad?"
"Water evaporates and goes into the sky, then it condenses high up in the sky to form clouds."
"What's 'evaporates' and 'condenses,' Dad?"
"It means the water turns into gas and then turns back into water."
"Why does it do that, Dad?"

You get the point. But why do we get frustrated when children question things like this? We often cut the conversation off by saying, "Well, that's just the way it is!" Or, we may even retreat by saying, "Because I said so, that's why!"

We know that children do this because they're naturally curious. Curiosity is "a desire to know; interest leading to inquiry." Children are unpretentious enough to expose their own ignorance. Adults get frustrated because repeated questions force us to think and come to a point where we don't know the answers. We discourage young people from "asking too many questions." Why is it that people who ask several questions seem to annoy us? Although asking questions temporarily reveals our ignorance to others, or forces us to admit it to ourselves, it's an essential habit we need to develop for success in the long run.

If there's one secret or magical formula that will help you learn higher paying skills more quickly, it's the ability to ask great questions. You need to continually ask questions to understand causes and effects, and to comprehend relationships between processes. You need to ask questions to understand human nature and what motivates people. Most importantly, **you need to question yourself** to understand why you do the things you do and how you can do them better. This chapter presents some methods for asking those types of questions.

Food For Thought

The late Will Durant, a very accomplished writer and historian wrote, "Education is a progressive discovery of our own ignorance." Sometimes, the people we honor as the wisest are not those who have all the answers, but **those who ask the most significant questions.**

For example, in American and European cultures, Socrates is honored as one of the wisest people of all time. His wisdom is detailed in Plato's *Dialogues*. Read the following passage where Socrates and Phaedrus discuss the merits of a speech given by Lysias:

> Socrates: "Answer this question yourself: What do adversaries do in the lawcourts? Don't they speak on opposite sides? What else can we call what they do?"
> Phaedrus: "That's it, exactly."
> Socrates: "About what is just and what is unjust?"

Phaedrus: "Yes." [...]
Socrates: "And won't whoever does this artfully make the same thing to appear to the same people sometimes just, and sometimes, when he prefers, unjust"
Phaedrus: "Of course."
Socrates: "And is it really possible for someone who doesn't know what each thing truly is to detect a similarity–whether large or small– between something he doesn't know and anything else?"
Phaedrus: "That is impossible." [...]
Socrates: "Could someone, then, who doesn't know what each thing is ever have the art to lead others little by little through similarities away from what is the case on each occasion to its opposite? Or, could he escape this being done to himself?"
Phaedrus: "Never."

(*Plato: Complete Works*, 1997)

Socrates didn't attempt to present himself as intelligent or wise. Rather, he insisted on his own ignorance and posed question after question to increase his understanding. His questioning habit effectively taught others because it compelled them to reexamine their own reasoning and assumptions.

You learn more from what people ask you than what they tell you. *Other people will learn more from what we ask them than what we tell them.* Your questioning skills will cause you to reexamine your own beliefs and premises for what you think. This is ripe territory for learning and growth. Consider this: when a newly-hired employee asked her manager why he hired her over the other candidates who applied, the manager said it was because of the questions she asked during the interviews!

The Anatomy of a Question

A *question* is defined as: "An expression of inquiry that invites or calls for a reply; to ask, to seek. A sentence in an interrogative form, addressed to someone in order to get information in reply." (*thefreedictionary.com*)

For our purposes, let's define a question differently, "An inquiry meant to reveal causality, assumptions, and understanding; a catalyst in learning and development."

Asking a question reveals your curiosity. Yes, it takes some courage to ask people questions because asking is an admission that you don't know something. Remember what Will Rogers said, "Everyone is ignorant, only on different subjects."

The ability to ask questions then, originates from curiosity–a desire to know and understand–combined with a little self-confidence and humility to seek information from other people.

You know that questions typically begin with one of these words:

Why, How, What, Who, When, Where

The most powerful words in this list are **why, how,** and **what** because they usually require more explanation to answer them. They're **open-ended** questions. It seems that you ask "why" questions to determine motivation for someone's actions, and "how" questions to determine a process—the way or method they used to do it. **Who, when,** and **where** are usually answered with short, one-word answers (closed-ended questions). Closed-ended questions mainly give you *information*; open-ended questions give you *understanding*.

Many of the questions you ask are meant to discover cause and effect:

- How did he win the election?

- If I pour this chemical into that tank, what will it do?

- Why did she quit her job?

- Why does he always treat me like that?

- Why am I unhappy at my job?

- How can I make more money?
- What the heck?

Challenge: Digging for Discovery

Below, you'll find some events and examples of questions that might determine cause and effect for those events. Create some questions of your own that might help reveal the cause that created each event. For now, don't worry about trying to answer the questions.

Event #1: The computer froze up! I can't get it to do anything!

- A possible question to discover the problem: *What were you trying to do when it happened?*

- List other questions you can ask to determine why the computer is broken:

Event #2: I'm going to quit my job and start my own business!

- A possible question to discover his motivation: *Why would you leave a secure job when the economy is so bad?*

- List other questions to ask to determine his reasons for quitting:

Event #3: She was able to increase her sales figures by 50% last month!

- A possible question to learn what she did so well: *How did she accomplish that?*

- List other questions you can ask to learn how she increased her sales numbers:

Questions Are Habit Forming

You'll find that an effective question naturally leads to more insight-producing questions. This question-asking momentum is a great tool for problem-solving. Here's a series of related questions to demonstrate how one good question leads to several others:

- How can I get better work and income?

- What is my definition of better work?

- How much income do I want and need?

- How can I make more money with the skills I already have?

- Do I need new skills to make more money?

- Which new skills should I develop?

- How can I learn these new skills?

- Who can help me learn those skills?

- When will I get started?

The point of asking several successive questions isn't just for the sake of asking questions. This routine will help you focus and identify the information that you *really* want, the answers which are the most valuable to you.

Asking great questions will make you a great conversationalist. Being able to establish common ground with coworkers, potential employers, and business clients will help your career and earning potential. In your conversations with other people, especially in professional settings, spend more time asking questions and listening to their answers than you do talking. Don't be afraid to ask questions about things that may seem obvious. Assuming we already know something may lead to errors and wasted effort. It's better to be certain.

Challenge: Your Own Work and Income Situation

Consider your own work and income situation. What questions could you ask and find answers to that would improve your job or business opportunities? Think of as many questions as you can, and write them down. The more specific questions you ask about your current situation, the more likely you'll be to find a path to improve it. A few examples are provided to help start you off:

- Why am I not making as much income as I want?

- How can I make more money?

- What type of job would I enjoy?

- Which businesses are doing well these days?

- How are those businesses doing well in a tough economy?

- List some other questions you can ask and answer to unlock more professional opportunities:

Summary:

- What's your definition of an effective question?

- How can asking effective questions help you develop higher paying skills?

- How can you improve your ability to ask more effective questions?

- Why do you learn more from what people ask you than what they tell you?

8 LEARNING ONLINE

We're going on three decades of having the Internet available to most people. It's changed the way we learn and communicate. You know there's as much garbage available online as there is good information. It's a great tool for learning if it's used right. It's a powerful resource when you know how to wade through the misinformation and find truly valuable facts. This chapter will cover the basics of effective Internet searching and other online resources for your professional development.

Start with Search Engines
One professor I had in a college history course loved to tell the story of a student who included bad information in a research paper he submitted. The professor tracked down the source of the information to a specific website. She discovered the content was created by some junior high school students as a class project. A college student used one of their website pages as a factual source of information for his research paper!

Our professor related this to us for the same reason I'm sharing it with you. Just because you find information on the Internet does not mean that it's credible. You must evaluate the authority of the information you find.

Search engines are programs that "crawl" websites on the Internet to create indexes of the information they find. Different search engines qualify and rank the same pages of information differently, so it's best to try your Internet searches in more than one search site. This improves your chances of locating what you need to know. The most popular, traditional search engines include: *Google, Yahoo, Bing,* and *Duck Duck Go.* Many sites and apps include search functionality up in the top menu.

How to Search More Effectively

When you enter a term into a search engine, how many pages of results do you sift through before you find what you need? Novice Internet searchers always seem amazed at the number of search results produced by search engines. Who has time to sift through 2.5 million search results? **That quantity of search results is actually not a good thing.** You need to modify your search queries to produce fewer, but more relevant results. Most search engines use special characters to yield better search results, but many people don't know about them. They're guaranteed to save you time and really tap the Internet's resourcefulness.

The first tip for getting more out of search engines is to simply put quotations around the exact phrase you want to find. This is called ***phrase searching***. It's one of the most effective techniques for improving your search results. Obviously, this won't change search results for a single word, but it will greatly improve searches for phrases of two or more words.

For example, if you entered: *rock climbers club*, search engines would return results for the words *rock*, and *climbers*, and *club*, whether those terms appeared next to each other or not. When you search for multiple-word phrases (without the quotes), you receive results for any one of those words in any order, or by themselves. Try it in a search engine and see for yourself. You'll see over a million results for web pages that have any ONE of those terms in them.

Now, take the same search terms, and put quotations around the entire phrase, like this: "*rock climbers club*" (include the quotation marks) and see what happens. The search engine displays results where all the words in the phrase appear exactly as they do within the quotation marks, and the order of the words is preserved. When you are looking for specific information and have only limited time, would you rather look through a million pages, or a few hundred?

Internet Searching Tips and Tricks
These vary based on the search engine:

- Put quotes " " around the phrase you're searching for, **"learn higher paying skills"**. This eliminates results where just one of the words in that phrase appears.

- Use the plus + sign in the search field, **engineering+jobs**; this will return results when only both terms appear together or at least close to each other.

- Use the minus – sign before a word to omit that term or subjects; **jobs–marketing**; this will omit any results with the term "marketing" from appearing in your "jobs" search results.

- Use the asterisk * sign to search for variations of a term; **instruct*** would return search results for all terms like *instruct, instruction, instructional, instructor*, etc.

- Search a single website for a specific phrase or term by including site:(name of the site) and then the search term. For example: **site:didactable.com money** would only return search results with the term "money" from the site, didactable.com.

- Use **CTRL+F** (*Control*+F) to find a term on a specific web page. This is not a search engine function, but a tool available in most Internet browsers.

- **Remember "Top-Ten"**– if what you're looking for doesn't show up in the first ten search results, then you should refine your search query with more specific keywords, phrases, or search operators. Remember that you want **quality** results, not necessarily *quantity*.

Challenge: Find Internet Resources for Learning

Using some of the tools discussed in this lesson, perform some Internet searches to find resources for learning skills you want to develop. For example, you could do some searches for "learn computer programming" or "start your own business." Remember that putting quotations around the specific phrase or idea you're looking for produces more relevant results. List some search phrases for things you want to learn:

-
-
-
-

Free Learning Resources on the Internet

In addition to using search engines to locate information on the Internet, there are many web sites and resources available to develop your knowledge and skills. Here are a few examples of some (free) tools available to you:

- *LinkedIn* Learning (linkedin.com/learning): This site is a collection of some very large online learning sites *LinkedIn* acquired (formerly

Lynda.com). You can complete free (or paid) courses and display your completions and certifications on your LinkedIn profile.

- *UDACITY* (udacity.com): Free online college courses; many are technical in nature. They add new courses each week.

- *COURSERA* (coursera.org): More free online college courses. The rumor is that several companies are paying to see who does well in these courses and offer them interviews for employment!

- *edX* (edx.org): Even more free online college courses. These courses sometimes offer an option to take a proctored test for about $100 to get college credit.

- *Udemy* (www.udemy.com): Most of these courses charge a fee, but not very much; some are free.

- *Project Gutenberg* (gutenberg.org): This online resource has over 36,000 free eBooks available to download to your computer or mobile device.

- *MIT Open Courseware* (ocw.mit.edu): MIT (Massachusetts Institute of Technology) has made the curriculum for many of its college courses available for free.

- Public Libraries and Databases: They offer many free online tools and resources to increase your knowledge, skills, and income potential. Do a search on your local library's website (or, for one on the other side of the country) and find the online resources section of their websites.

Challenge: Identify More Learning Resources

Use your Internet searching skills to identify other "free learning resources" for skill development or business opportunities. Bookmark a few websites that appear to have valuable, credible information about these skills or opportunities. Really dig deep to identify more well-researched and documented sites, not just popular ones that rank high in the search engines. List some of the free resources you found:

-

-

-

Online Certifications, Courses, and Programs

The Internet offers more formal ways to learn and get certified. No matter what skills you're trying to develop, or which degrees and certifications you want, there are multiple ways for you to get the education you need online. However, you generally have to pay for these programs. Most colleges have online programs available. Find the website for a college close to you (or, far away from you) and determine what online programs are available.

Other organizations offer online programs for professional development. You may want a certification within a specific industry. For example, do a search for "PMP certification" (Project Management Professional) or "CNA certification" (Certified Nursing Assistant). Perhaps you're an architect or builder who needs to add some "environmentally friendly" credentials to your services. Search for "LEED certification program" to see what's available online.

Online Communities and Discussion Groups

You can learn from connecting with experts online. *LinkedIn* has active groups focused on thousands of different professional interests and industries. (See linkedin.com/directory/groups/) You can look for communities or forums on other sites you visit. On most sites, there are places at the bottom of the page where you can submit comments or questions. I've used this tool to submit questions to authors and other experts who read the articles. You'll be able to get (free) guidance and information from experts by using these online discussions.

Challenge: Start an Online Discussion

- Find a website, blog, or online forum related to your professional interests. Use your Internet searching skills to locate a few. If necessary, create a personal profile on those sites. Then, post a question about something related to that website's subject.

- Be sure to follow discussion forum etiquette. Search the site to see if that topic has already been discussed or if the question is already answered.

- And don't go "off-topic" in a discussion (or "thread" as they're sometimes called) by talking about an unrelated subject.

How to Qualify Information on the Internet

Anyone can create a site on the Internet. Just because you find something online, even if the information is from a professional-looking website, it doesn't mean the information is credible. If you plan on using the Internet to improve your professional knowledge and skills, you'll need to ensure that what you learn is authoritative information.

Here are things to consider when evaluating the credibility of online information:

- **Ask, "Who wrote it?"** Credible Internet authors should have information about their credentials on an "About Us" or author summary page. Is this person someone who has real experience, certification, or accomplishments in this area? Or, is he just a self-certified expert offering personal opinions?

- **Is there factual support?** Does the article refer to credible sources and established facts? Does it link to other trustworthy sites? Do other credible writers or sites refer to this information?

- **Judge a book by its cover.** You can *partially* evaluate the credibility of an Internet resource by looking at the website itself. Is it designed professionally? Is there a lot of other related content? Are the grammar and spelling correct? Does the website have a way to contact the owners and authors? A true professional should ensure the content is edited correctly and the site is well-designed.

Challenge: Evaluating Online Credibility

Perform another Internet search on a topic related to your professional interests. As you click through links to various websites, consider the following questions:

- Which sites contain trustworthy information?

- Why do they seem to be more credible?

- What sites don't seem as credible, and why?

- What can you find out about the authors or owners of each website?

- Which of the authors would you trust to give you the most credible information? Why?

A.I. – Pros and Cons

This section is an addition to the 2025 edition of the book. There wasn't any need for it originally when it first went on sale (in 2011). A.I. is an acronym for Artificial Intelligence, but **I think it would be better represented by the term, "Aggregated Information."** The AI tools have been at work for years scraping information and data from the internet and databases. Unknown to most people, is that many of the leading AI apps have had teams of thousands of people typing in and creating responses to common search queries. Millions of books have had their text scanned into or made available to these systems. (*Google Books*, *Amazon Kindle*, etc.)

Programmers have worked to combine that aggregated information that gets assembled and then displayed when someone enters a search request. Some computers can program other computers. There are sites and apps that create graphic design and artwork based on terms and parameters people type in. Music in all known or even new genres is being created by computers. What does all this mean to your relevance? How should AI influence your learning and professional development? While this continues to be sorted out in the upcoming years, consider these questions:

- If your professional marketability relies on gathering, organizing, and presenting information, how much of a threat do these programs and systems present to your career?

- What are you capable of doing that these AI systems cannot do?

- How can you secure your employment and income as these systems get better at collecting and combining information?

- These AI systems are basically plagiarizers: taking others' intellectual property or creations, revising them in some degree, then presenting them as their own. If your career depends on intellectual property protections (think patents, trademarks, brands, copyrights, etc.), how can you better ensure your work is unique and profitable?

I think there's a subtle agenda in play here to create a system that the public is **led to believe** is more intelligent than any one person individually, and smarter than all of us collectively. Remember that at best, these systems rely entirely on probability, not certainty. At the two extremes, there are people who think everything is controlled by outside determining factors, that everything is acted upon, and others who believe there's free will, identity, choice, and self-determination. You'll see that as people surrender their accountability to these systems, the systems will make disastrous mistakes that make us all question if the benefits have justified the risks.

Summary

- You can leverage the benefits of the Internet to learn while avoiding its traps and distractions.

- Use Internet search engines to find valuable information about an industry, to identify free learning resources, to help build your business, and advance your career.

- Internet searching is much more efficient when you use specific phrases within quotation marks (" ") to eliminate useless search results. You can also improve your Internet searching abilities by using other search operators like an asterisk (*), plus (+) or minus (-) signs, and site-specific searches (site:...).

- You need to evaluate the credibility of information you find online. Determine if the authors are trustworthy by evaluating their credentials. Discover whether other credible sites link to them or not.

- You need to stay informed of how the changing landscape of so-called Artificial Intelligence might affect your education, career choices, and job security. (AI = *Aggregated Information*, both correct and incorrect information.).

SECTION 3: WHAT SKILLS TO LEARN

Sections 1 and 2 answered the questions of **Why** and **How** to learn higher paying skills. Section 3 presents information and exercises to help you learn what some of those skills are. These apply to any career path you choose. Another important point: You can strengthen and improve each one of these skills no matter how much progress you've already made.

Remember to complete the challenges in each chapter or come up with your own ways to apply what you're learning. Make all your learning active learning

9 LEARN TO WORK

**"The problem with this generation is they don't know
how to work."**
- Some guy in the 1920s, and another guy in the
1930s, and many more guys in the 40s, 50s, 60s, 70s, etc.

How often have you heard someone say the people of
a younger generation just don't know how to work? I
continue to hear it a lot in the conversations I have with
business owners and recruiting teams. Younger people
certainly resent that stereotype, even if a few of them do
resemble it! The intergenerational conflict might come
from how the definition of work has changed over time.

I'm sure there's *something* everyone works very hard at.
It might not be something they're paid for. It might not be
something that another person recognizes as work. **If
there's no overlap between what you think is work and
what someone else recognizes as work, you'll never be
paid for it.** It's very rare that anyone will pay you for having
fun all day. Although some self-help books and career
coaches tell you to only do work you love, that won't pay
the bills. We'll revisit this idea in the chapter on job
hunting. This chapter will clarify your definition of work,
why it's important, and how you can strengthen your own
work ethic.

**"The only place where success comes before work is in
the dictionary."**

What is Work?

> *"Now that ain't workin', that's the way you do it,*
> *You play the guitar on the MTV.*
> *That ain't workin', that's the way you do it,*
> *Money for nothin' and your chicks for free.*
> *We got to install microwave ovens,*
> *custom kitchen deliveries.*
> *We got to move these refrigerators,*
> *we gotta move these color TVs."*
> - Lyrics from *Money for Nothing*, by Dire Straits

Work is defined as: **"Performing a task requiring sustained effort or continuous repeated operations; to exert oneself physically or mentally especially in sustained effort for a purpose, or under compulsion or necessity."** (*Merriam-Websters.com*) There's also a scientific definition of work used in physics defining it as the amount of force applied to an object over a specific distance. I like that the first definition includes exerting oneself mentally as well as physically.

Some of the contention about who does or doesn't know how to work may come from a sense of entitlement each group perceives in the other. Entitlement means someone feels that they're owed something by another person or group of people. A sense of entitlement causes someone to think they shouldn't have to work as much as another for what they receive. Don't ever think you're **entitled** to better work and pay. **Earn** them! Abraham Lincoln, in his second Inaugural Address said, "*It may seem strange that any men should dare ask a just God's assistance in wringing their bread from the sweat of other men's faces.*"

What's Work Ethic?

You've certainly heard people talk about **work ethic.** Work ethic means placing a high value on the importance of work. It also includes the necessary discipline and persistence to ***start and finish a task***. The work you do is a sacrifice of time, an expenditure of your energy and effort. In a few more pages, we'll look at strategies to strengthen your work ethic and how to demonstrate that ability to potential employers.

Finding better work may mean you need to broaden your idea of what work looks like. Broadening that definition can present new ideas about what skills and talents you should develop. You'll discover new opportunities for career development that you've likely not thought of before.

And remember what my father told me after I worked a very long day in the summer sun and heat: "God gave you a brain so you wouldn't have to sweat so much!" Determine the difference between *working hard* and *working smart*. They're both good, but you need to find the balance between them. You can work very hard but make little progress. And if some smart person has great ideas but never works to realize them, they'll never get anywhere professionally or financially either. Always ask if there's a better way to get things done without sacrificing quality in your work.

Challenge: Your Definition of Work

Write out your own definition of work. Then answer these questions:

- How do you think your definition compares to others' definitions of work?

- Why is it important that your definition of work mostly matches an employer's definition of work?

- What's the difference between working hard and working smart?

Why Work?

"I love work. I can watch it all day long!"
- One of my old bosses

Most people work primarily for a paycheck. But working also has other benefits:

- People **learn** while they work. Even mundane labor like digging invites workers to find more efficient ways of doing it. For example, taking smaller shovels full of dirt can be sustained a lot longer than full, heavy shovel loads.

- You can develop friendships while you work.

- You can learn from other more experienced people while you work.

- Your work gives you a sense of place and importance.

- You can increase your sense of self-worth and others can develop a higher opinion of you based on the quality and quantity of work you do.

- Building a reputation and track record of work accomplishments makes you more desirable for better jobs and promotions.

One reason to **learn to enjoy work** is because it spares you the discouragement and waste of idleness. Idleness is being inactive—not having opportunities or being unwilling to work. Being idle, whether by choice or not, brings a sense of insecurity, unimportance, and unworthiness. It's closely associated with being lazy. Laziness kills your professional reputation and better career opportunities.

In the Christian New Testament, there's a story told by Jesus about a man who needed workers to help harvest his field. He found people to work starting early in the day and agreed to a certain wage for their day's labor, so they went to work. Later, he went and found more people to help with the harvest, agreed to a wage for their labor, and they went to work too. Late in the day, he found some people standing around and asked why they hadn't gone to work that day. They told him no one hired them. With harvesting still going on in his fields, he agreed to employ them to help finish the job. When the harvest was all gathered in, he paid his workers their agreed-upon wages. The people who had labored all day felt cheated because the laborers who came to work later got the same amount of pay as those who started early.

Aside from the lesson in the story about honoring an agreement, there's the fact that the people who stood around most of the day were haunted by the lack of work. The uncertainty of whether or not anyone would hire them must have felt intolerable. The thought of returning home to their families with no earnings and that their labor wasn't wanted must have caused embarrassment. The people who got hired early for an acceptable wage avoided the worry and frustration of idleness. They felt a sense of purpose and importance and enjoyed the confidence of knowing they'd return home with wages and bread that day.

Challenge: Work's Importance to You

Write down your answers to these questions:

- What things do you like about work?

- What have you worked hardest to accomplish in your life?

- How would an even stronger work ethic improve your life?

Strategies to Develop Your Work Ethic

You've learned about what work is and why it's important. Remember that a strong work ethic will increase your chances of getting better work and more compensation. Now read about some strategies to *strengthen* your work ethic:

Imagine the results of your work. You might have a stack of papers that need to be read and sorted through. Or, you might have a blank document in front of you on the screen and you're trying to think of what to write. (Perhaps you're trying to write about strategies to develop a strong work ethic.) There might be a whole warehouse that needs to be inventoried. You might have several acres of grass to cut. You might be looking at several thousand lines of code that need to be debugged. You might be facing the sheer horror of a whole day of calls and meetings to attend. Whatever work you're facing, it might seem impossible to complete before you begin it. Envisioning what the finished product looks like, how you'll feel when you've accomplished it, and considering what rewards await on the other end of your task will help you start and maintain your efforts.

Plan and prioritize. Have you heard anyone say, "Plan your work, then work your plan?" The accomplishment you want needs to be translated into how you'll do it. A well-defined goal is written down and answers the questions of what, why, when, who, and how. Define what you need to accomplish in very specific terms. Give it a time limit. Identify any possible obstacles or distractions that will prevent you from accomplishing your work. **Plan to do the most *unpleasant* things first**. It will make the remainder of work you need to do seem easier or more enjoyable. You can also **do the most *important* thing** first as you start your work. The most *important* thing to do may also be the most *unpleasant* thing to do! Some people like to pick a simple, easy task to do first because it helps them start building some momentum for the day.

Get started. Someone wrote that, "The secret to getting ahead is getting started." And an ancient proverb says, "A journey of a thousand miles begins with a single step." A disproportionate amount of fuel is spent by airplanes and rockets in the first few minutes of their flights. They're trying to accelerate and develop momentum against the gravitational pull. You'll find that your work is the same way. It's hard getting started...breaking the gravitational pull of inaction or other distractions. Simply begin it. Put one foot in front of the other and keep at it. Someone also said, "Stick with a task until it sticks to you."

Break it up. What you read earlier about an effective way to study applies to work and productivity as well. Effort can be sustained much longer if it's divided up into intervals. The quality of your study and work improves when you regularly pause to catch your breath, both physically and mentally. Pacing yourself is closely related to this. Ask yourself if you're more of a work horse, or a race horse. Race horses sprint, and it's exciting to watch and makes money for the winners. They couldn't maintain that pace for very long though. Work horses move more slowly, but they can sustain that effort over several hours. Both approaches to work have their benefits, and your preferences may be different for mental effort or physical labor.

Get help. Working with someone, especially if you can carry on intermittent conversations while working, makes the task much more endurable. Find others who are aligned with what you need to do. This also permits specialization. Your friend or coworker might be better at one part of the job than you are, and you have talents that make you better at another part of a job than him. Working with someone increases the quantity and quality of your work when there's some good-natured competition and encouragement.

Reflect on your accomplishments. People you work for might say thanks or compliment you on your work, but it's rare they'll ever fully appreciate how much effort you put into getting something done. *You'll know though*. Take a minute to look at the results of your work. Perhaps it's something you designed, created, cleaned up, repaired, built, composed, programmed, or you may have managed other people to get something done. Whatever you did and did well, tell yourself, "Good job!" Take photos of the project—before and after if possible—to provide motivation and confidence for the next project you must do.

Challenge: Your Own Work Ethic

Think about a time where you had something important you needed to get done, *but had a very tough time trying to keep yourself focused enough to finish.* Answer these questions:

- What was the reward for getting that project done?

- What were the consequences going to be for not getting it done?

- What were you doing or thinking about instead of the work that needed doing?

- What should you have done differently?

Now consider a situation *when you worked very hard to accomplish something*, and answer these questions:

- Was that project easy?

- How were you able to focus, stay committed, and finish the project?

- How can you produce the same effort, focus, and commitment on future projects?

Make Yourself Indispensable

Indispensable is defined as, "absolutely necessary; essential." Another site adds more to that definition: "If you say that someone is indispensable, you mean that they are absolutely essential and other people or things cannot function without them." (*Collinsdictionary.com*) Indispensable people are first in line to get promotions and pay raises. They're last in line for layoffs.

I've worked with many independent contractors in the corporate world. Contractors are people who aren't brought on as employees but they're hired for a specific project or timeframe. Most of them are very good and committed to the work they do. Their livelihoods depend on productivity and reliability. They're relatively easy for a company to let go of (fire) without the legal headaches of terminating regular employees. This fact makes most contract employees very keen on becoming indispensable to the companies they're working for.

One large international company went through three rounds of layoffs in the five years I worked with them. Several regular employees lost their jobs. The team of contractors I worked with didn't lose anyone. They constantly proved their worth to the company and enjoyed more job security than thousands of long-term, regular employees had.

One contractor was incredibly good at graphic and multimedia design. However, her creativity was offset by not always being available when the company needed her. And she was also great at procrastination. Did she get let go when these layoffs happened? No! Her skills were so good that she proved to be **indispensable** to this company. "*They are absolutely essential and other people or things cannot function without them.*" Realistically, *you* need to be a reliable work horse, even if this designer got by with being an unpredictable race horse. Your indispensability to an employer or company can deteriorate if you don't keep doing things to maintain it.

How to Make Yourself Indispensable

How do you make yourself indispensable to an employer, company, or to customers? Here are a few ideas:

Do *great* work. Like the talented designer you just read about, if it's very difficult to find anyone who can do stellar work, you'll become indispensable to a company. But don't test their patience. The more skilled and specialized you become, the more companies will want to hang onto you. That's basically the message of this entire book!

Do a *lot* of work. Maybe the work you do doesn't always have to be homerun, star-quality work. It may be sufficient to produce reliable, consistent work that's just fine for your employer or customers. They may value a productive stream of "good enough" work more than intermittent, highly-creative work. Discover what they value most.

Inconvenience yourself. This means being there when customers or employers need you. I retained jobs when others lost them because I'd respond to an email on the weekend. It didn't take much effort or time to do it and it communicated my commitment to helping that client succeed. Others would work late, even overnight sometimes, when a client faced a tight deadline. This doesn't mean you allow employers or clients to abuse you. It means that when your boss, company, or customer are experiencing a real problem or tight deadline, show up and do what you can to help them out. Realize that sacrifices for other people are really investments in your relationship and reputation.

Challenge: Indispensable People

Who have you known who was indispensable (absolutely necessary, essential) to a company or to their customers? Answer these questions:

- What work did they do that was essential?

- Was it talent or commitment that enabled them to do that work? Perhaps a bit of both?

- What can you do to be more like those people?

Life is Work

We've discussed work in the context of jobs, careers, and business. Art is work. Athletics are work. Academics are work. Marriage is work. Parenting is work. Friendships are work. Good health is hard work. Playing and recreation are work in their own ways. But the alternative to all these isn't ease, it's idleness.

When you learn to improve your work ethic, you'll improve every area of your life. So don't simply resign yourself to working more, as if it's some punishment, get excited about it. You can work your way through and out of most problems you face in life, especially professional challenges.

Summary

- Work is a task requiring sustained effort or continuous repeated effort. Work ethic is placing a high value on the importance of work. It includes the necessary discipline and persistence to start and finish a task.

- You can improve your work ethic by envisioning the satisfaction and rewards from your efforts, by setting goals, by planning and prioritizing your work, and by simply getting started. You can get help and regularly reflect on the accomplishments from your work.

- You'll become indispensable to employers, companies, and customers by performing both a large quantity of work and high-quality work. You'll prove to be very valuable by inconveniencing yourself occasionally and putting others' needs before your own.

10 LEARN TO SOLVE PROBLEMS

Here's another skill worth learning, one that will never become obsolete and one that will do wonders for you in any career path or business: **problem solving!**

As you consider which skills to learn to get better work and income, add effective problem solving to your list. Everyone has problems and welcomes solutions to them. Businesses have problems that cost them money. Your ability to solve these problems will help them save or make more money. If you establish a reputation as a money-saving problem solver, companies will want to hire you.

Consumers have problems. Every day they purchase products and services they believe will solve their problems. You'll discover many professional opportunities when you identify problems people face and then offer solutions. This chapter discusses problem solving skills that can increase your marketability and income.

A Simple Fix

We usually employed college students as bindery assistants in the print shop where I worked. They oversaw finishing, packaging, and delivering all the printed materials that our company produced. We printed and numbered thousands of invoices and business forms then stapled them into covered booklets. As a convenience to our customers, we wrote the range of numbers of the forms contained in each booklet on the cover. The problem was we used a felt-tipped pen to do this and after writing the numbers on hundreds of books, our writing got very sloppy. Sometimes we miscounted and wrote the incorrect numbers on the booklet covers. To correct our mistakes, we crossed out the incorrect numbers and rewrote the correct ones. This made the booklets we delivered to our customers look messy and unprofessional.

One of those employees created a few label templates using *Microsoft Excel*, which calculated the correct form numbers and printed out nicely-formatted labels. We simply stuck these to the booklet covers. This solution not only looked much more professional, it saved the print shop time and money too. This was a simple fix to an annoying problem.

You can get better work and income as you develop your ability to effectively solve problems. Problem solving can be broken down into the simple steps of identifying the problem, determining the causes of the problem, inventing solutions to the problem, and then implementing these solutions to get rid of the problem.

What's the Problem?

According to *Merriam-Webster.com*, a problem is defined as: *a source of perplexity, distress, or vexation*. The word originates from the Latin term meaning *an obstacle*. Some problems businesses and organizations face include:

- Not enough income to pay for expenses

- Lawsuits or a deteriorating public image

- Rising costs of fuel, supplies, or materials

- Political instability and war

- Environmental pollution and regulations

- Finding and retaining talented workers

- Trying to please investors or shareholders

- Unproductive employees

Some problems individuals face include:

- Not enough income to pay expenses
- Cost and availability of healthcare
- Foreclosed homes
- Rising costs of advanced education
- Difficult family relationships
- Unsatisfying, poor-paying jobs and careers
- Unemployment

Challenge: Problems, Problems!
List your top-10 problems, then list the top-10 problems that either your employer or your customers face. If you're currently unemployed, try to list the top-10 problems one of your potential employers may face. You'll refer to these lists later in the chapter. What are your top-10 problems?

1.

2.

3.

4.

5.

6.

7.

8.

9.

10.

What are your employer's, potential employer's, or customer's top-10 problems?

1.

2.

3.

4.

5.

6.

7.

8.

9.

10.

As you can see, there's no lack of problems surrounding you, your business, or your employer. This exercise isn't meant to discourage you. It's meant to help you see that the opportunities to help solve problems are infinite! Now, let's look at how to turn problems into opportunities.

What IS Problem Solving?

You understand what a problem is and that problems create many opportunities. Businesses, organizations, and people look for solutions to their problems. Just about every product or service you see represents a solution to a problem. For example:

- Mobile phones solve the problem of not being able to communicate with people regardless of their locations.

- Computers solve the problem of not being able to create, store, replicate, and share information quickly and inexpensively.

- Cars, airplanes, and other transportation methods solve the problem of getting ourselves across great distances in a short amount of time.

- Healthcare professionals help solve problems with our bodies.

- Programmers and technicians solve problems with our computers or machinery.

The more complex a problem is, the more people are willing to pay to have it resolved. If you want to receive more money for the work you do, **you'll either need to solve more problems, or solve more difficult problems than you do now.**

How to Solve Problems

Problems usually come from more than one cause. There are many variables which can combine to create problems. Sometimes you can solve a problem quickly, but usually it takes a lot of time and study to correct it. Generally, there are a few things that need to happen for both simple and complex problems.

1) Identify the Problem. Don't dismiss the seemingly simple step of defining the problem. Many people only complain and don't take time to define their problems more specifically. "My job stinks!" and, "I can't get a job!" are not constructive problem descriptions. **Understand that a well-defined problem is half solved!** Look at these examples of poorly-defined versus effectively-defined problems:

Poorly-Defined Problem: I hate my job!
Effectively-Defined Problem: I don't receive the amount of money, recognition, or appreciation I deserve for the work I do.

Poorly-Defined Problem: Our sales are bad!
Effectively-Defined Problem: Gross sales for our two top products are down 10% compared to this time last year.
Poorly-Defined Problem: I can't get a job!
Effectively-Defined Problem: I've submitted 20 online applications and told my network of friends I'm job hunting, but no one has called to discuss or offer me a position.

Poorly-Defined Problem: I don't have enough money to pay our bills!
Effectively-Defined Problem: I need $500 more each month to cover our mortgage, utilities, food, and car payments.

Did you notice that poorly-defined problems usually take the form of complaints? More effectively-defined problems include **specific descriptions of the situation**. This specific information gives you a starting point for solving the problem. The poorly-defined problems (the complaints) immobilize you. They make you think you can't do anything about them. Effectively defining problems empowers you and puts you in a better position to resolve them!

Challenge: Revisit Your Problems
Earlier, you listed your top-10 problems and the problems your employer or customers face. For this exercise, define each one of these problems with more specific details. Remember that effectively defining problems enables you to solve more of them. Write out your top-10 problems (from the last challenge), **but define them more effectively**:

1.

2.

3.

4.

5.

6.

7.

8.

9.

10.

Next, write out your employer or customer's top-10 problems, **but define them more effectively.**

1.

2.

3.

4.

5.

6.

7.

8.

9.

10.

Consider this: How do you feel about your problems after you've taken time to define them more effectively? Do they seem more manageable?

2) Determine What's Causing a Problem. Another element of problem solving is determining what's causing or contributing to the problem. If you've taken the time to effectively define a problem, then you've probably uncovered details that reveal causes of the problem. I'm repeating this because it's so important to understand: **a well-defined problem is half solved!**

Understanding some basic laws of nature will help you identify the causes of a problem. Sir Isaac Newton described natural phenomena observed in nature with his *Laws of Motion*. One states that everything remains in its current state or path of motion unless it's acted upon by some outside force. Another one of Newton's observations is that for any and every action there is an equal and opposite reaction.

Science and philosophy discuss the concept of causality, or trying to determine the relationship between events and their effects. What all this talk of science and philosophy means is that when anything happens (good or bad), there are reasons for it. Nothing occurs *ex nihilo* (that's Latin for *from nothing*). With some study, experimentation, and inquiry, you can find out the cause or reasons for anything! After you discover the causes or reasons for anything, then you can take measures to change or control it.

It seems obvious that applying these principles of nature to problem solving is appropriate when you're trying to determine why a car, computer, or machine isn't working. What about when you're trying to discover why a certain client, supervisor, or customer behaves a certain way? People's behavior is not subject to these material laws. So how do you solve "people" problems then? There are psychological explanations for peoples' behavior as well; they have a motivation or reason for anything they do. We'll discuss this more in the chapter on persuasion.

Identifying the cause of a problem will depend heavily on asking effective questions. The easiest way to begin identifying the cause of a problem is to ask (drumroll):

"What's causing the problem?"

That's an obvious question, but many people fail or forget or refuse to ask it. Too often, we accept problems or circumstances as they are and don't take time to think about them. We often choose to complain about problems instead of doing anything productive to resolve them. Asking this first question will lead to other questions that help discover the cause of a problem. Get into the habit of asking these types of questions to better identify the possible causes:

- What's causing this?

- When has this happened before?

- Why is he/she behaving that way?

- Why am I acting this way?

- Why did he make that same mistake again?

Challenge: Who or What's to Blame?

Go back to the last challenge activity (where you defined your problems more effectively) and simply ask, "What's causing this?" for each of the problems you've listed. See if you can identify–or at least guess–the primary cause of each problem.

3) Determine the Solution. When you've defined a problem and its causes, then you determine how to solve it. Remember the natural and psychological laws we referred to earlier–that there's a cause for any problem that occurs, or a reason for the way people behave. Problems can be simple (a single cause) or complex (multiple causes and variables). You can fix or reduce a problem by affecting its cause(s), no matter how difficult it may be. If you change or get rid of the things that are causing the problem, you get rid of the problem. While that seems like common sense, it's not common practice.

Identifying a solution to a problem doesn't necessarily mean that remedy is practical or cost-effective. As you try to find solutions to problems, brainstorm as many solutions as possible so you can eliminate those that are less practical or too expensive to implement.

Example 1
Problem: Employees won't follow the new operating procedure.
Cause(s): They don't know how to do it or, they don't have any incentive to follow it.
Possible Solutions: Develop a training program for employees to learn the new procedure. Reward and recognize employees who follow the procedure. Discipline or terminate employees who will not follow the procedure!

Example 2
Problem: Our largest customer has not ordered any products from us in the last two months.
Cause(s): We delivered their last order two days late. They buy from our competitor now.
Possible Solutions: Offer them a new discounted pricing structure if they order from us. Offer them free 2-day shipping on future orders. Find another customer to offset the lost revenue.

Example 3
Problem: I keep getting job interviews, but no actual job offers.
Cause(s): I may expect too high of a salary or employers may think I'm over-qualified.
Possible Solutions: Resign myself to working for a smaller salary. Convince potential employers that I'm committed to and passionate about this work and industry, that's why I've been in it for so long!

Challenge: Solutions, Solutions!
Brainstorm several possible solutions to the top-10 problems you've been working with throughout this lesson (your own and your employer's). You should have already identified the possible causes for these problems, so finding a solution means determining how to eliminate or change the cause(s) of each problem.

4) Implement the Solution. Defining a problem, its causes, and possible solutions by themselves won't solve the problem. Your problem-solving skills need to result in plans and actions to remedy the difficulty. Applying the solution to a problem may take the form of a new product, service, process, or habit. As you and your business build a reputation for solving problems, you'll find that more people will depend on you for solutions. (Remember, make yourself *indispensable*!) They'll pay you more and pay you more frequently for those solutions.

Select the most realistic or cost-effective option from your list of possible solutions to the problem. Set those plans in motion: create a new process, procedure, product, or service. You may need to get permission from your supervisor before you change anything. If your solution is a new product, you may need to get financing before your business can develop and market it.

Understand that to solve problems, you must *do something*—you must implement a solution. There are people who simply *have ideas* about how to solve problems, and there are people who *actually solve them*. What kind of person will you be?

Challenge: Action Plan

- What are you *going to do* to solve your first few problems from your Top-10 list? When?

- What are you *going to do* to solve your company's first few problems from their Top-10 list? When?

Summary

- Great problem-solving skills begin with effectively defining the problem. The more detail you provide to describe a problem, the closer you'll come to finding a solution.

- Remember that **a well-defined problem is half solved!**

- "For every action, there's an equal and opposite reaction." A problem occurs because a combination of factors create it. When you determine the causes of a problem, you're empowered with knowledge to change or control it.

- A solution to a problem is simply an intervention or putting a stop to the causes of that problem. You should think of several solutions to a problem because some of them may not be practical or cost-effective.

11 LEARN TO COMMUNICATE CONFIDENTLY AND CLEARLY

One of the first things potential employers or clients notice about you is how well you communicate. To communicate means to give information to another person in the form of words, sounds, gestures, writing, or signals. Even when you have great knowledge or helpful information to share, it does no good if you can't express it clearly and in a way that others have confidence in your message.

Communicating confidently includes:

- Actively listening to and observing the expressions of other people to ensure you understand them.

- Using words, tone of voice, and body language that come naturally and comfortably to you.

- Being specific and clear about what you want other people to understand.

- Being entertaining, or informative, and engaging when you speak.

- Communicating your ideas and feelings in a way that leaves a memorable impression on others.

- When you communicate confidently, people want to listen to and remember what you say.

Communicating confidently **does not** include:

- Being argumentative, pushy, loud, arrogant, or rude.
- Taking over conversations and doing all the talking.
- Speaking artificially, that is, using words, voice, or gestures that aren't natural to you.
- Using communication to mislead or manipulate.

Why do you want to be able to speak confidently? Do you feel your lack of confidence is holding you back from a promotion or pay raise? Or, is it because people who communicate well seem to have a big advantage over the people who don't?

If you're like me, there have been many times—after meetings and conversations with supervisors or coworkers—that I wish I said something better than I did. I missed out on some opportunities early in my career because I didn't feel confident saying what I really thought. I've learned some important lessons since then, and they've helped me become a more confident communicator.

As you improve your ability to communicate your ideas to people you work with, it may be the single most important career skill you ever develop. If you think about it, some of the highest paid people in your business are probably not the people who have the most knowledge or technical skill, but people who communicate the best.

Everyone can improve their careers when they learn better communication skills. This chapter presents several strategies to communicate better in professional situations. Most of the things here also apply to communicating better in social settings and personal relationships. Apply as many of these things as possible to increase your opportunities for better work and income.

Learn to Listen Well

When we consider confident communication, we usually think of speaking. **Listening skills should come first.** As you learn to listen better, you'll learn more from other people. You'll make a better impression on the people you meet and work with. Listening well shows people you value them and their information. If you listen closely to instructions, you demonstrate you want to do things right. Here are some strategies to improve your listening skills:

- **Look at who's speaking.** Do you remember a parent or teacher ever saying, "Look at me when I'm talking to you!" If we don't look at people who are speaking to us, they think we're not listening. Looking at something else while they speak communicates, "You or what you're saying isn't that important." The next section will go into more detail about the right amount of eye contact.

- **Give visual indications you're listening.** You want to show your attentiveness in other ways. These include non-verbal reactions like nodding your head in agreement or to show you understand. Your listening reactions might also include hand gestures like a thumbs-up to show approval or a fist-pump to show pride or accomplishment.

- **Acknowledge or restate what they're saying in your own words.** This ensures you're receiving the message the speaker wants to communicate. Speak carefully so you don't make what they say seem unimportant when you restate it.

Example:

Boss: "I need you to finish that report and then get going on the other three. I want them on my desk by the 15th."

Employee: "I'll get the first one finished and sent to you tomorrow, and then have the other three done a week from Friday."

- **Reflect understanding AND feelings.** If someone speaks to you with any emotion, it's a good practice to acknowledge their feelings, even if you don't sympathize with how they feel. If someone is angry or afraid, speaking calmly can help de-escalate the situation. Again, you must be careful because if someone is stressed or panicked and you respond unemotionally, it might communicate their feelings are trivial and unimportant. Reflect their emotion in what you say to show you understand. Your facial expressions can communicate much of this without having to say anything. Smile, frown, look surprised, or sad, whatever's appropriate for the conversation.

Example:

Employee: "I turned in that report she was waiting for, but now I have three more I have to prepare!"

Coworker: "Wow! You did so much work on that report, and now she wants three more in a week?"

- **Put the phone down.** Better yet, put it away. You want people you're speaking with to feel they're the most important thing at that moment. If they're interrupting something important to speak to you, acknowledge them with your full attention, if only for a moment. Say something like, "I want to hear what you have to say. Let me finish this up so I can give you my full attention."

- **Write things down.** A manager offered me a job after a series of interviews and said she chose me over the other applicants because I took notes during our interviews. When someone speaks and gives you information or details about an event, write the important points down on paper. Or, if you prefer taking notes with your phone, tell them that you're making some notes on your phone, so they don't think you're ignoring them.

- **Try not to interrupt.** Interruptions happen all the time. In personal conversations they're sometimes acceptable, especially if you're asking the other person to clarify something. In professional situations, interrupting people makes the interrupter look inconsiderate. Raise your hand or hold your hand up in front of yourself to signal you need the speaker to pause. Some people in meetings or conversations take up too much time. Sometimes they need to be interrupted for the sake of time or in favor of others who also have something to say. Just speak carefully when you do it.

  Example: "I hate to cut you off. What you're saying is important and we'd like to get that information from you in an email or in next week's meeting. Let's take the few minutes we have left to discuss these other agenda items..."

- **Don't try to solve their problems.** "You just had a whole chapter on problem-solving, but now you're saying don't try to solve people's problems?" Problem-solving is a valuable career skill when people *want* you to solve their problems. In conversations, if people are describing or even complaining about their problems, they shouldn't expect you to fix those problems for them. They're mainly looking for some sympathy or your perspective on their challenges. But they usually don't want or need you to jump into the situation and make it all right. Listen to them with some empathy for their struggle. Ask questions that help them see the challenge in a manageable way. Offer help and encouragement, but let them determine their own solutions to their own problems.

Challenge: Listening Even Better

These strategies are just a few suggestions for listening well. Answer these questions:

- Aside from those things, what's something else you can do to be a better listener?

- How do you plan to develop that ability?

- What benefits will come to you as you become a better listener?

- What personal and professional *consequences* will come if you don't become a better listener?

Strategies for Speaking Confidently at Work

Remember, communication skills are what employers want most in potential employees. And effective, confident communication skills are one of the most important abilities great leaders can have. Here are some strategies to improve your communication in your professional life.

- **Speak Honestly and Clearly.** Speaking honestly at work means a lot more than just telling the truth. It means talking in a way that reflects your personality. You want to be clear about what you think and feel. Try to avoid only saying what you believe other people want to hear. Communicate messages consistent with your thoughts, feelings, and authentic self. Don't use words or phrases that you wouldn't use naturally. Some people think they can sound more impressive by using big words or jargon, but they usually come across as being fake or insincere.

  The same goes for the kind of voice you use when you talk to coworkers. Don't try to fake confidence or certainty by talking louder or more forcefully. Just talk in your natural voice in a steady pace. Being honest about what you say and how you say it will help you feel more confident. You won't feel the fear and insecurity that come from being artificial.

- **Don't Be Insensitive.** Being honest doesn't mean you should be rude or insensitive when you talk to people. Remember that if you don't agree with someone's ideas, you can still find the good in those ideas, call it out, and then present your reasons for why there might be another option. Don't attack people personally.

  Keep your conversation focused on the ideas and what's best for the situation. Doing this will help you speak more assertively. Focusing on ideas as opposed to the people presenting them will help you express your own ideas more confidently. **Be more concerned more with** *what is right*, **as opposed to** *who is right*.

- **Talk More Confidently by Talking Less.** Do you know people who talk a lot but who say nothing important? Maybe they're just trying to pretend and even hide their lack of real knowledge and experience. They think that having *an opinion* about anything makes them an authority on everything. Don't be that kind of person. Realize that people who talk too much end up being ignored or avoided by other people.

  You want to speak only when you have something worthwhile to say. If you practice this habit, people will listen to you more because you've developed a reputation of giving a lot of thought to what you're saying. As your reputation of saying meaningful things gets more widespread, you'll feel more confident because you know people listen to you and are interested in what you have to say.

  Don't say anything more if a meeting has gone overtime. As the time approaches for the scheduled meeting to finish, it's best not to keep speaking. Save your other ideas to include in a follow-up email or to be discussed in another meeting. When the time is getting close to end the meeting, people start looking at their watches, they pack their bags, or they may just get up and leave. The person speaking has a hard time keeping people's attention and sometimes even makes the participants mad if it looks like the meeting is going to go over the allotted time. You won't feel confident speaking in these circumstances, so it's best to not say anything more.

- **Do Your Homework.** You can speak more confidently at work when you have actual data to back up what you say. Again, simply having an opinion on something doesn't give you any authority. But when you have real information to share, you're seen as more credible. When you're seen as more credible, it helps you speak more confidently. When you know, in advance, what a meeting or conversation is going to be about, take time to research those subjects so you can feel prepared to talk confidently about them. Remember where you got your information from so you can refer to it when asked.

- **Maintain the Right Amount of Eye Contact.** I took an interpersonal communications course in college and the instructor asked me to come talk to him after class. He asked me to tell him about my career plans and what my professional goals were. As I talked, he never looked at me. He kept looking around the room. He deliberately avoided making any eye contact. When I stopped talking, he asked how that made me feel as he looked around the room while I spoke. I told him I felt he wasn't listening, that it made me uncomfortable.

He said he was listening and repeated several things I said to prove it. But he pointed out that *people need to know* we're listening to them. We need to make regular eye contact to communicate they have our attention. He noticed that I rarely looked people in the eye when they talked to me but he knew I listened to what they said. He challenged me to make a deliberate effort to make better eye contact with people when they spoke. He emphasized it was a crucial, non-verbal communication skill I needed to develop. Don't overdo it though. 100% eye contact during a conversation is creepy. Aim for about 75% eye contact while people speak with you. In meetings, it's easy to focus on your friends or close coworkers when you're speaking, but you need to make sure to have eye contact with as many people as possible. Try to look at each person for just a second or two while you're speaking. Some people may not look you in the eyes, but that's OK, just move to the next person.

Making eye contact with as many people as possible will cause them to be more engaged and pay more attention to what you say. Even though many people are afraid of having other people look at them when they're speaking in front of a group, I've found that looking at people one at a time makes me feel a lot less nervous. Instead of focusing on one big, intimidating group of people while you talk, you see one person at a time and your presentation feels more like a personal conversation.

- **Speak More Confidently Using Stories.** When you communicate your ideas using personal experiences, or by using stories which reinforce your ideas, you speak more confidently. You become less focused on yourself and more engaged in what you want people to hear and understand. Using personal experiences to represent your ideas helps you become less self-conscious. You're less worried about what words to use and what other people think of you.

Think of experiences you've had in your career that taught you important lessons about the work you do. Write out those experiences and practice telling them to other people. Keep a simple work journal where you record the details of new experiences and the lessons you learned.

- **Speak Professionally, not Pretentiously.** Remember that what you talk about and the words you use need to be appropriate for the workplace. Sometimes people forget where they're at and use inappropriate or offensive words. You'll feel more confident speaking to people if you're certain they're not going to be offended by something you say. Practice respect and diplomacy when you talk to other people.

Don't use unnecessary long words or confusing terms. Some people try too hard to use "two-dollar" words and acronyms. An acronym is an abbreviation formed from the initial letters of other words and pronounced as a word. Like C.R.M. = **C**ustomer **R**elationship **M**anagement. Certain jobs and industries use several acronyms that are meaningful to people in those industries, but other people may have no idea what those terms really mean. It doesn't impress people if you use too much of this language. If you need to use an acronym, be sure to say the entire phrase out first, pronounce its acronym, and then you can refer to it from then on using its acronym.

For example, some people in business might say, "S.O.P" which means "Standard Operating Procedure." If you're in a meeting where everyone may not know your job or department's acronyms say, *"Our Standard Operating Procedure, or SOP, says we should..."* That way people will understand what you're talking about. Knowing they understand your vocabulary will help you feel more confident.

Also avoid using corporate-speak, also called *businessese*, which is using words and phrases that are meant to sound professional, but are unnecessary and confusing. Many people say "utilize" in the business world when "use" works just as well. Do an internet search for the terms *"corporate-speak"* or *"businessese"* to see more examples.

- **Use the Three Magic Words.** We established that talking confidently does not mean you have to say something about everything. One tool to communicate effectively are the three magic words. What are they? **"I don't know."** Yes, those *are* the words. Talking confidently means feeling assured about what you say. Trying to fake certainty or knowledge about anything is obvious to most people. It doesn't work. An important step to learning to talk confidently is admitting when you don't have something meaningful to say.

  Becoming comfortable saying you *don't know* means that you've learned how to pick your battles. You reserve your speaking for those times when you really know what you're talking about. Focus on the quality of what you say instead of the quantity of your talking. It means being courageous and confident enough to use those magic words. Having the self-confidence to say them earns others' professional respect. Over the next few days, see how many opportunities you have to say, "I don't know." It's a fun experiment and an important part of talking more confidently when you **do** have something to say.

- **Focus on One Single Thing.** Identify one thing you want the other person or people to know, remember, feel, or do when you finish talking to them. It's not as mechanical as setting a goal for every conversation you have, because your communication will seem unnatural or even manipulative. And most conversations are unplanned, like meeting someone in the hall or at a store, so it's hard to predict those. As often as possible, think about the conversations or the opportunities you'll have to speak in advance. Determine that single thing you want them to remember, do, or feel because of what you say. It should be something clear and very simple.

You may want to leave people with a general feeling or impression about an idea or about yourself. Keep in mind that, "people don't always remember what you say, but they rarely forget how you made them feel." This sense of purpose when you communicate helps to diminish your feelings of uncertainty. Your communication is clearer and your confidence is more impressive when you identify your desired outcome for conversations.

Challenge: Where to Start
Answer these action-planning questions to begin improving your workplace communication skills:

- Which one of the strategies you learned about seems like the most applicable to you right now?

- When will you have an opportunity to practice it, and with who?

- Which one of those strategies feels like it would be *the most difficult* for you to do?

- That most difficult strategy is probably the best opportunity for improving your communication skills. How can you make it a habit?

The Secret of Great Impromptu Speaking

Impromptu speaking is also called thinking on your feet, extemporaneous speaking, or speaking off-the-cuff. Being able to think and speak well on your feet is one of the most important professional skills you can get. It's even more valuable than formal public speaking ability because you have many informal, conversational talks for every one formal public speech you deliver. The definition of impromptu speaking according to a few different sources is:

- "Not prepared ahead of time: made or done without preparation." (*Merriam-webster.com*)

- "Made or done without previous preparation; suddenly or hastily prepared; improvised." (*Dictionary.com*)

- "The impromptu speech is given without any preparation, notes or other additional materials; it is a spontaneous reaction to the topic at hand." (*Speech-guru.com*)

Do you know people who are great impromptu speakers? People with great impromptu speaking skills are the ones who make the sale and who get elected. Those who communicate well on-the-spot get promotions. But people who speak so well in just about any situation *without any apparent preparation* have a very closely guarded secret. So, what is it? How do these people say such impressive things off-the-cuff? How do they come up with things to say that advance them professionally and socially without any preparation?

They prepare! They're always preparing for the next opportunity to talk. You may think they had no time to prepare, when ***they were very well-prepared for that moment.***

But what about the definition of impromptu speaking, "not prepared ahead of time" and all that? Those definitions of impromptu speaking are deceitfully wrong. They must be part of a conspiracy by competent extemporaneous speakers to make everyone else think they'll never get that communication skill. Now that their secret is out, how should you go about preparing for these unexpected, unplanned-for speaking opportunities?

You can become a great impromptu speaker yourself with a simple habit or strategy. This is a habit I've used for several years while I've sat through boring classes, long meetings, and dull lessons. It puts the time to good use. It's this: Always be imagining a conversation, or thinking of an intelligent comment, or composing a speech whenever you can. In the next meeting you're in, ask yourself, **"If I was called on to say something, what would I say right now?"**

Anticipate conversations and discussions before they happen, then **plan what you might say.** Next, and this is very important, imagine or visualize yourself saying what you've thought of in that conversation. Imagine seeing and hearing yourself standing up in that meeting to share your thoughts. Do these things over and over, every day. It will help you develop your ability to talk confidently. People will be more attentive to you as you **learn to prepare for comments and conversations you're not supposed to be prepared for.**

Challenge: Preparing to Speak

- What's the next class or meeting you'll attend?

- What questions will be asked, or what topics will the group discuss?

- If you're called on to answer or speak, what will you say about those topics?

- How can you prepare for what you'll say?

- How can you make sure that what you say is natural and conversational, without sounding like it's memorized?

LEARN HIGHER PAYING SKILLS

Speaking Professionally on the Phone

Don't dismiss the need to improve your ability to communicate effectively on the phone and during virtual meetings. Not seeing someone's body language leads easily to misunderstandings. Those misunderstandings can ruin careers. Remember these important points when speaking on the phone to people in work environments:

- **Listen**. All the principles for listening well that you've already read about (and practiced) apply to phone calls too. You can't listen well to the other person when you talk most of the time. Practice restating what they've said in your own words. Ask additional follow-up questions to make sure you understand.

- **Speak clearly and just a little bit slower than usual.** People generally speak between 150 and 200 words per minute. We can usually comprehend speech at an even higher rate, but that also depends on the ability to subconsciously read lip movements and hear vocal inflections. Phone calls place us at a disadvantage because we can't see the other person's face and read their lips like we can face-to-face. And phone call quality doesn't allow us to hear all the vocal nuances that often communicate a lot of information during in-person conversations.

- Restate the details of any decisions, actions, commitments, or appointments made during your conversation before ending the call. **Examples**: "Great. I'll review the proposal you sent over, track my edits to the document, and get it sent back to you before the end of the month." And, "OK, I'll come to your office downtown, next Wednesday, at 11 AM."

- **Always identify yourself** by first name on incoming calls: "Hi, this is Maria." Or, "Hello, this is David." On outgoing calls, if it's someone you haven't spoken to before or someone you speak with infrequently, **identify yourself by first and last name, then the company you're with.** Sometimes it might not be on behalf of a company but you can briefly mention what you're calling about.

Examples: "Hello Chen, this is Reina from Company Solutions." Or, "Hi, this is Rebecca Davis calling about the request for bids on your upcoming construction project."

- **Be prepared to leave a voicemail message.** I've seen and heard people embarrass themselves because they've messed up leaving voicemail messages on clients' or customers' phones. They weren't prepared to leave a recording and stuttered, cussed, or even mistakenly said, "I love you," when the other person's voicemail beeped and started recording. What's worse is those mistakes are recorded and often replayed for the amusement of other coworkers. Avoid those embarrassing situations that might kill a professional opportunity. Expect and prepare to leave a voicemail message every time you make a business-related call. Have a few notes jotted down on paper to get the details right.

- If you're using wireless service, **ensure you're in a place with good signal strength** BEFORE making any important calls. Having to ask a coworker, customer, or client, "Can you hear me now?" will kill the goal of your conversation very quickly, especially if you have to ask more than once. Check your signal strength and go to someplace quiet before you make those important calls.

Writing Professionally

Learning to communicate confidently and clearly includes writing that way too. So many people, even high-up executives, send email messages or documents that contain misspellings and generally poor writing. These same people speak very well and articulately. They'd do better dictating everything they wanted to say and then sending that out. You're responsible for your own written communication. Recognize that misspelled words or unclear writing can leave an unfavorable impression on the people you do business with. That lack of attention might kill your work and income opportunities. To minimize that risk, practice these writing strategies:

- **Don't use text-ese or emojis** in your workplace communication. Text-ese includes that ever-growing collection of acronyms and shorthand people often use in messages (*BRB, BTW, LOL, IDK,* etc.). It works fine for communication with friends and family, except that when you're in the habit of using that language enough, it's likely to spill over in your work communication. Not everyone understands these abbreviations and text-ese will make you look immature and inexperienced.

- **Save your email messages or documents as drafts,** then come back and re-read them. Looking at them after a pause of a few minutes or hours will help you spot problems with your writing and correct them **before** they're sent off. This is also a great practice if there's any emotionally-charged issue in what you've written about. You can better ensure you're not insulting anyone or making the situation worse with poorly-chosen words and statements.

- **Use the spelling and grammar checks** built into most word processing and email programs. These programs aren't foolproof. They sometimes miss certain words and grammatical errors. But generally, they do a good job at cleaning up and correcting your writing. Be careful to proofread because these programs won't find problem words like *you're* vs. *your*, and *its* vs. *it's*, or *then* vs. *than*.

- **Read your writing out loud.** We read with our eyes much quicker than we can with our mouths, but slowing down is a good thing when proofreading. Some things that look good on paper or on the screen don't sound right when we hear them. Ears are better tools when it comes to proofreading than eyes are.

- For highly-important messages or documents, **get someone else to read and review them.** When your professional reputation is on the line, if your resume is being put in front of a potential employer, or a big business deal depends on the clarity and professionalism of a written message, you must have someone else read them. You don't want someone who's too kind and worried about hurting your feelings when they review your writing. You want someone who's competent as a writer and critical of your documents.

Challenge: Presenting and Public Speaking

This chapter on learning communication skills has gone on for a while and we haven't even gotten into more formal communication like public speaking or presentations. 99% of your communication in the work world will qualify as the more informal conversations, meetings, phone calls, and emails you've already learned strategies for. The Internet has vast amounts of free information about how to do professional presentations and how to be an effective public speaker when you need that. Based on your current job needs or goals, complete the following exercises:

- Using the internet, search for *"strategies for successful presentations."* Create your own short checklist you can use when you need to prepare a formal presentation for work, a client, or for school. Call your list *"10 Things to Remember for a Successful Presentation."*

- Do the same for public speaking, in the event you need to give a more formal speech to a group of people. Search for *"tips for successful public speaking"* and make a custom list for yourself called, *"10 Things to Remember for Successful Public Speaking."*

Dale Carnegie, known for his highly-successful programs to make great public speakers and presenters out of shy people told them to "perfect their natural manner of conversation and carry that to the platform." He taught that you should speak *with* people, not just *at* them, especially at the podium. So, as you work on these professional *conversation* skills in this chapter, apply those same things to any *formal presentation or speaking* you do.

Challenge: Confident Communication Case Studies
Think of examples when people missed out on important opportunities because of poor communication. Answer these questions:

- What consequences did those people experience because of the way they communicated?

- What should they have done differently?

- What can you do to ensure you don't make the same mistakes with your professional communication?

On a positive note, think of people who had more professional opportunities and success because of their clear, confident communication.

- In your opinion, what did they do to communicate so well?

- Do you think their communication skills are something you can develop yourself? Why or why not?

- What can you **do** to start developing those same communication skills?

Summary

- Being a great listener is more important than being a good speaker.

- Be yourself when you talk: be honest without being insensitive to other people.

- Focus more on the quality of what you say instead of the quantity.

- Be prepared by studying and researching. Develop some *authority* to speak on a topic, not just an opinion.

- Use stories and experiences to communicate what you want people to understand and remember.

- Learn to talk diplomatically at work; don't say things that might offend people.

- Be prepared for those times you need to speak with no preparation. *Anticipate* what will be talked about in advance, become knowledgeable on those topics, and *expect* to be called on to say something about them.

- You should follow the proven strategies for successful phone and written communication. These are just as important as your spoken communication.

- While formal presentations and public speaking are important skills to have as you advance in your career, the more informal conversations, meetings, emails, and phone calls will have a larger impact on your job opportunities and potential for advancement. Focus on your day-to-day communication skills and you'll become a more confident communicator in more formal settings.

12 LEARN TO DEVELOP PROFESSIONAL RELATIONSHIPS

Have you known anyone who got a good job simply because of friendships or relationships they had with someone else? Most of the time this is unfair and unfortunate. Underqualified people get put into positions they didn't earn or deserve. Their lack of capability increases the workloads of other people who must work with or for them. On the other hand, many well-qualified people can't seem to get hired for positions they deserve. There's a gap between the right people and the right jobs. Professional relationship building and maintenance can bridge that gap.

What is an Effective Professional Relationship?

A relationship is an association between two people. They communicate and participate in some type of common activity or purpose. Professional relationships are associations you develop while doing your work or business. Professional success in terms of relationships means treating other people (above and below you) as you want to be treated. You can transform your perspective on professional relationships by focusing on other people.

Get Outside Yourself

After I finished college and moved to Denver, Colorado, I signed up to attend a networking event for people who worked in the corporate training industry. I hoped to meet someone who could help me land a job or get my resume into the hands of a hiring manager. I put a small stack of my freshly-printed resumes into a professional-looking folder and went to the event.

When I arrived, I saw all sorts of people mingling around the room. It only took a few seconds for someone to come up to me, introduce herself, and then slip a business card into my half-closed hand. "I'm an independent consultant," she said. She continued, "I offer businesses a way to maximize their employees' performance...blah...blah...blah!" She asked who I worked for. When I said, "I'm actually just out of college and looking for a job," her excitement turned into disappointment and she said, "Well, good luck! Glad to meet you!" Then she turned away to scout the room for other opportunities.

It was that same story over and over again at that networking event. Everyone I met seemed to be obsessed with generating new business leads. I realized later that most of these folks were just as unemployed as I was. They were trying to spin their circumstances in a more positive way. I didn't have the chance to give a resume to anyone.

If I *had been* gainfully employed and in a position to do something for any of these people, I don't think I would have wanted to anyway! I wouldn't have been inclined to help them because it seemed they were only interested in helping themselves. Keep that in mind as you seek to develop professional relationships with other people. Focus more on what you can do for them rather than what they might do for you.

We established in an earlier lesson that **what** you know is at least as important, if not more important, than **who** you know. However, getting better work and income will depend heavily on the professional relationships you develop. Connecting with people in business environments seems to come naturally to some people. The rest of us need to work at it just like any other skill development.

What Have You Done for Me Lately?

So much of the "networking" advice we read or hear about takes a very self-centered approach to building relationships. Some experts tell you to always be on the lookout: give your business cards to people and constantly evaluate their potential worth for helping your career or business. You've certainly met people like this. Their self-serving interest in you isn't very well masked. The real message of their behavior is, "How can I use you to make more money or accomplish my own goals?" How does this make you feel? If you have an attitude like this as you meet people in professional settings, they'll feel the same way.

Think, "How Can I Help YOU?"

You can avoid the reputation of a self-serving person by focusing on what other people want and need. Introduce yourself to new people with the expectation of helping them out in some way. Now realistically, you *do* want other people's help in your career or business development. The help you need will seem to come effortlessly, even magically, as you concentrate on serving instead of being served.

How to Develop Professional Relationships

You can adopt an effective, natural approach to developing worthwhile relationships by cultivating a few simple habits. Here are some proven methods for helping you connect with people.

- **Develop a trustworthy reputation for hard work**. Other people need to feel you are worth knowing. You can cultivate this feeling in other people by maintaining your integrity, by fulfilling commitments. Keep high expectations for your work and never present anything you wouldn't be glad to receive yourself. Don't miss appointments and be on time.

- **Listen to, and learn from others**. Do people who talk all the time really impress you? They seem like they're trying to conceal their ignorance or compensate for personal insecurity. Understand that everyone is an expert on some subject. Ask questions, then wait for and pay attention to their answers. Ask successful people about their achievements and what advice they have to offer. Don't be afraid to share information about your own abilities and achievements, but do so conservatively and only when asked.

- **Learn to say, "Thanks!"** Sincere gratitude is in short supply across the business world. You can do a lot to solidify relationships by thanking people for their help. Yes, thank your boss for the opportunity to work on a special project. Thank coworkers for their contributions to the team. Thank your customers for their business. I know a president of a company who, when he started his own business, sent Christmas cards to some past clients. One of the clients received the card and called him because of it. Their conversation led to a million dollars' worth of new business for his upstart company. All this from a card sent as a thank-you for past opportunities.

- **Send business their way**. Instead of interrogating people for job opportunities or sales leads, find out what type of work *they're* looking for. Ask for their business cards instead of forcing yours on them. You'll find that people are more likely to remember you and your business when you *try to help them out first*. When you send business opportunities their way, they'll feel more inclined to reciprocate and do the same for you.

- **Go to lunch**. Something about inviting other people to lunch and paying for it has a real professional payoff. It's not just your generosity that does it. When you leave the workplace to go eat at a restaurant, it's a more comfortable environment. People are more open and relaxed. You get to know each other more completely. In addition, the feelings of organizational hierarchy and the buyer/seller relationship diminish. This leads to more open conversations than those in the workplace. (See *Never Eat Alone* by Ferrazzi & Raz)

- **Keep in touch**. Find reasons to keep in contact with people you meet professionally. You can call to ask how their jobs or industries are doing. You can send an email with a link to a page or article they may find helpful. The relationship is only as good as the communication that exists between you, so make sure the channels stay open.

Challenge: Rescue Your Professional Relationships
First, invite a coworker or customer to lunch and pay for it. Then, focus on listening and understanding how their job or industry is doing.

- Who will you take to lunch?

- What will you ask them?

Challenge: Maintain Professional Relationships

Think of three people you've met professionally, perhaps a few you haven't contacted in a while. Get in touch with them again. Write down their names, how you'll contact them, and what you'll ask them about:

1 –

2 –

3 –

Keep Track of Your Connections

Ideally, you'll remember people's names and faces, but it's not easy when you meet dozens or hundreds of people in professional settings each year. There are tools available where you can record contact information for those you meet. There are paid software services like *Salesforce.com* or *Sage Act* that keep track of customer information.

LinkedIn works well (if people accept your connection requests) because they tend to keep their contact information updated their profiles. They usually include a photo of themselves that will help you remember them.

Most people use their phone, but that can get difficult separating professional and personal contacts. And you don't want to accidentally butt-dial anyone if your career success depends on what they think of you. I maintain a simple spreadsheet of professional and business contacts to keep track of their information outside of my phone.

Summary:

- Connecting with people professionally should be more about what you can offer them than what they can do for you. The more you focus on helping people in their careers and businesses, the more likely they are to help you in return.

- Cultivate a hard-working, trustworthy reputation.

- Listen to and learn from other people.

- Say "thank you" more often.

- Send business and opportunities to other people.

- Take others to lunch.

- Keep in contact with the people you meet.

13 LEARN HOW TO PERSUADE PEOPLE

What's the difference between persuasion and manipulation? Someone once made the distinction by saying manipulation is when people visibly comply with a request or demand, but in their minds and hearts they're unwilling or resentful. Persuasion, on the other hand, is when people do what they are told or asked willingly, with no resentment. (See Dr. Robert Cialdini's books on persuasion and influence.)

For example, let's imagine I approach a stranger and tell him I was out of money and very hungry. I then ask him if he could give me ten dollars to buy some lunch. This man may choose to give me the money out of pity or he wants to feel good about himself. If he gives me the money willingly, you could say I *persuaded* him to give it to me.

Now, let's imagine I went up to another guy and told him I would beat him up if he didn't give me ten dollars. If this guy gave me ten dollars, you can't really say he was persuaded. He was intimidated or compelled to give it to me. He gave me the money unwillingly. I manipulated him to give me what I wanted, but certainly not what he really wanted.

Everyone needs to persuade other people. A baby persuades his mother to pick him up and feed him. Children persuade parents or teachers and vice versa. Job hunters must persuade recruiters and hiring managers to interview them and present a job offer. Sales professionals try to get people to purchase products or services. Political candidates try to persuade voters for their votes and contributions. Even representatives of non-profit organizations need to persuade donors to sponsor their work or charity.

As you work to develop career skills, you should learn how to effectively and appropriately influence other people. This chapter discusses what effective persuasion is and how you can employ a simple pattern to persuade people.

What is Persuasion?

Persuasion is communication meant to influence people to believe or do something **willingly**. It's presenting someone with reasons and incentives for taking action. Getting people to do something when they're unwilling or resentful is not persuasion–that's called compulsion or manipulation. Manipulation is defined as, "controlling by artful, unfair, or insidious means, especially to one's own advantage." (From *Webster's Encyclopedic Dictionary*.)

Have you ever been lured into buying something you really didn't want? The crafty salesman may have congratulated himself on making a sale and earning a commission. However, he failed to realize the damage his reputation and the company's reputation suffered by tricking you into a purchase. The ability you need to develop *is not some trick* to get people to do what you want. The truly valuable persuasive skill you need is the ability to influence people *to get what they want*, what's really in *their* best interest.

People seem to be increasingly aware and resistant to any sales or psychological "trick" that's used on them. Although we may not understand the approach being used on us, we sense when we're being manipulated and influenced against our own wills. At the same time, we appreciate being told about opportunities or beneficial products and services. We prefer to be in control of our own decisions and how we spend our time and money.

As you work to develop your persuasive abilities, you should always allow your respect for people's autonomy to override your desire to make a point or to close a sale. While you may have to delay or sacrifice what it is you want from this person, it's the best option for building your professional reputation and self-respect.

Types of Persuasion

In European and American cultures, many persuasive approaches originate from Ancient Greek philosophy. Aristotle classified persuasion into three different categories:

- **Logical**: Rational arguments or reasons presented to convince people of some opinion or fact; appealing to thought or reason. Use facts, figures, and data.

- **Emotional**: Appeal to feelings to influence people; communication intended primarily to evoke sentiment like sympathy, fear, excitement, or desire. Use stories, portraits, or anecdotes.

- **Authoritative**: Appeals to position, power, or credibility to influence other people. Use quotes, your own credentials, or credentials and authority of other people.

Which one of these is the best approach to use when you're trying to persuade people? It depends on the person and the circumstances. If you cannot determine whether a person or audience is more logical or emotional, then use a combination of these types of persuasion to generate the most influence.

Why People Do What They Do

Think about your motivation for anything you do. Your motivation will fall into one of these simple categories:

1. You do it because you want to **get or keep something good**, profitable, or pleasurable.

2. You do it because you want to **get rid of or avoid something bad or painful**.

Remembering this will help you persuade other people and it can help you motivate yourself.

Challenge: Watch Commercial TV
Spend a few hours watching TV, but instead of trying to avoid commercials, pay special attention to them. Answer these questions:

- What is each commercial trying to get you to do?

- What problems do their products or services try to solve?

- What persuasive approaches are they using to convince you?

How to Appropriately Persuade People
There are many different approaches for persuading people. The route you take depends on who you're talking to, what it is you're convincing them to believe or do, and what the costs or risks are for doing what you ask. What follows are some critical elements you need to understand as you try to persuade people. This information is generally based on *Monroe's Motivated Sequence*.

1) First, persuade yourself. In all the sales books and sales training programs I've read, I've never seen a persuasive approach that begins with convincing yourself first. They should. If you're sincerely convinced of the benefits of a product, service, course of action, behavior, or decision, then your ability to get someone else to agree to that increases many times over.

The latest trend in selling or influencing people isn't really a trend at all; it's being honest and transparent! Before you ask someone else to do something, ask yourself if it's in their best interest, or your best interest. Perhaps it's something that's in both of your best interests; a win-win! Before you ask them to purchase anything, ask yourself if you would buy that product or service at that price. Before you ask for a job or promotion, look at yourself objectively and determine if you're truly qualified for it.

2) Get their interest. Once you've convinced yourself of the benefits of what you're trying to persuade someone else to do, begin by getting their interest and attention. Getting someone's attention can be tricky because you usually have to interrupt whatever they're doing. What you offer them had better be more important than what they were doing to begin with. You need to consider who they are, what they're interested in, and what channel of communication you're using to connect with them.

The basic rule to follow for getting someone's interest and attention is to present some benefit right up front. As Dale Carnegie taught, "Talk in terms of the other person's interests." Get their attention by sharing a relevant story or ask a question they can't resist answering like, "What don't you like about your job?" Or ask, "If money wasn't an issue, what would you do with your time each day?" Here's a question you can ask someone who owns their own business: "How did you get started in your own company?" To discover their needs, ask "What problems are you and your business dealing with right now?"

The key here is that you *get* others' attention by *giving* them your sincere, undivided attention. Get them interested in what you have to say by talking about what they have to gain.

3) Identify a problem or opportunity for them. When you listen to what people have to say–as you identify what motivates and concerns them–you can understand their problems better. The more familiar you become with their industry or personal goals, the more influence you have with them. What is causing them pain and difficulty in their careers or business? What opportunities and payoffs are available to them? Some examples of identifying a problem or opportunity for someone else include:

- "There are a lot of companies in this industry that aren't profitable right now."
- "You'll never be happy working in this position for that amount of pay."
- "You seem like you'd be happier if your business was making a little more money."
- "Getting into arguments with other team members certainly won't help your career."

When you identify a problem or opportunity for someone you're trying to persuade, it introduces a feeling of *cognitive dissonance*. Cognitive dissonance is "psychological conflict resulting from incongruous beliefs and attitudes held simultaneously." (Merriam-Websters.com) To define that more simply, it's when we try to mentally reconcile the conflict between ideas that we know are true but seem contradictory.

Identifying a problem for someone creates a desire to get something good or avoid something bad. Describing problems or opportunities that someone faces sets up a feeling of expectation in their minds. It positions you to explain solutions and potential opportunities for them.

4) Present a fulfillment to their wants or needs. Show how your skills, your company's products and services, or a change in someone's behavior will help them get what they want or need. This is where you need to present your logical, emotional, or authoritative information to convert them to your proposed solution. An effective approach is to ask them how *they* think your solution will help them solve their problem or fulfill their needs. They essentially convince themselves at this point. They persuade themselves more effectively than you ever could!

5) Get people to commit and take action. When someone seems convinced that what you've offered or proposed can get them what they want, invite them to take action. It may mean asking them to work on changing their behavior, purchasing your product, or signing a petition. Tell them exactly what they need to do and ask them to make a verbal or written agreement to do it.

Challenge: Other Forms of Persuasion

- List some other ideas about how you could persuade someone to do something. Remember that just getting people to do something isn't persuasion if they comply resentfully.

- Think of the last time someone persuaded you to do something. How did they do it?

- When was the last time you persuaded someone else to do something and why did it work?

Persuasion in Action – Example 1

Read through this scenario where Carlos, a computer technician, tries to persuade Marie, his manager, to give him a raise. Carlos made an appointment with her. After asking how she was doing, he asked an attention-getting question:

Carlos: "I scheduled this meeting with you today because I wanted to ask you a question. How can I help you get more work done and make our team more productive?"

Marie: "Well, I'm not sure Carlos. You always work

really hard and are a great member of the team. You'll stay late when our work is piled up. What is it that you have in mind?"

Carlos: "I've enjoyed being on the team and I'm glad that you appreciate my work. I've actually got a friend who works as a technician at another company. He says they're understaffed and they're looking to hire more people. He said that they pay about five dollars more an hour than what I'm making now."

Marie: "Do they pay that much? Are you thinking about leaving our company?"

Carlos: "Don't get me wrong, I really want to stay here on the team–working for this company–but a five-dollar per hour increase is some great money. With my daughter going off to college this year, I'd really like to have a little more cash to help her out. I did some research online and found that someone with my skills, certification and experience is paid at least a few dollars an hour more than I'm making now. Do you think you could get me a raise of a few more dollars an hour?"

Marie: "Well, let me see what I can do. I need to submit some paperwork to the compensation department and see if they approve a raise for you."

Carlos: "That would be great! If I can get that raise, you won't have to worry about me looking elsewhere. You won't have to go through the hassle of interviewing, hiring, and training someone new either. How long will it take to find out if Comp approves the raise?"

Marie: "If I get the papers submitted this week, it will probably take another week to hear back from them."

Carlos: "OK. Can I follow up with you at the end of next week then?"

Marie: "That will be fine."

Did you notice how Carlos effectively persuaded his manager to submit a request for his raise? He was honest and didn't manipulate. He influenced Marie by showing that her job would be easier if he could get a raise. Here are some other observations about this example:

- Carlos got her attention and interest by asking about what she wants and needs from him as an employee. Any supervisor would love to hear that question.

- Carlos hinted that Marie may risk losing him if he can't be paid more for his work. He presents her with a potential problem.

- Carlos made emotional and logical appeals. He wanted to help his daughter with her college expenses and he cited evidence that he's worth more than he's making now.

- He proposed a solution to the problem in the form of a question.

- Carlos constantly spoke in terms of Marie's needs and interests.

- He committed Marie to submitting the pay increase paperwork by asking another question.

Think of the example and answer these questions:

- What other things did Carlos do well to persuade his manager?

- What could he have done better?

- Do you think he was being manipulative by mentioning another higher paying job opportunity? Why, or why not?

Persuasion in Action – Example 2

Edward has been in business for about two years. His company provides landscape and lawn maintenance services for businesses and commercial properties. He got a call two weeks ago from Kate, the facilities manager for a large office complex.

Kate wanted Edward to give her an estimate for providing landscape maintenance services for her company buildings. She was dissatisfied with the current company. Edward set an appointment with Kate to follow up and discuss his bid. But she didn't seem as determined to find a new landscape company the morning that Edward met with her:

Edward: "I know you're really busy with all your responsibilities. I just wanted to follow up on your decision to get a new maintenance contract for the grounds here. What questions do you have about that estimate I sent you?"

Kate: "I got it and looked it over, but I really don't have any questions. Your bid was about $1000 more per month than our current provider though."

Edward: "We charge a little more to make sure you get reliable, consistent service. You said that the company you're using now failed to respond quickly to some broken sprinklers last month?"

Kate: "Yes, it was a mess. There was some flooding in the parking lot, and my director wasn't very happy when he saw all the wasted water."

Edward: "Your time is too precious to have to deal with problems like that. If you accept my company's bid and sign the contract for our services, you'll have peace of mind knowing problems will get taken care of right away. We're on-call 24 hours a day. In the long run, it will actually cost you less in terms of headaches and hassles to contract with our company. We can start as soon as next week. What will it take to get you to accept our contract?"

Kate: "Well, I need to run it by our director to get his approval, and then notify our current landscape company that we're terminating their contract."

Edward: "OK, can I call you later this week to see how it went with your director? I'll bring a copy of the contract for you to sign this Friday. I can meet on Monday to walk the grounds and create a maintenance schedule for you. How does that sound?"

Kate: "It sounds like a good plan to me."

Edward knew that Kate and her company would be pleased with the landscape services he offered. That confidence helped make him more assertive when asking Kate to approve the contract. Some other observations:

- Edward talked in terms of his potential client's concerns.

- From their prior conversations, Edward knew about the time sprinklers broke and flooded the parking lot. He let Kate talk about that event to convince herself of the need for a new contract.

- Edward presented her with a call to action; he invited Kate to accept the contract.

- Arranging to follow up is an effective persuasive practice.

Consider these questions:

- Did Edward seem pushy or manipulative to you?

- Do you believe that Kate agreed to the contract willingly?

- What would you have done differently to persuade Kate if you were in the same situation?

These examples are simple, realistic applications of persuasion. You'll develop effective persuasive abilities as you continually think and talk in terms of what others want and need.

Persuasion in a Nutshell

- **Speak to their heads**. Give them sound, logical reasons for making a certain choice.

- **Speak to their hearts**. Include a sympathetic description of those things that are causing them pain and trouble.

- **Be sure to describe** how their choice to do what you ask or purchase what you offer will bring them more peace of mind and pleasure. Provide details about the potential benefits.

Challenge: Your Turn to Persuade

Think of some people who you need to influence, then work through these questions to prepare an effective persuasive approach:

- Who do you need to persuade or influence?

- What do you want them to do or believe?

- How will you get their attention and interest?

- What is the problem or opportunity they face?

- What solutions will you propose?

- What commitment will you have them make?

- What actions do they need to take next?

Summary:

- Think of persuasion as helping people get what they want instead of getting them to do what you want.

- The most persuasive approaches include logical, emotional, and authoritative information.

- You need to be persuaded of something yourself to effectively persuade anyone else.

- An effective approach to persuading people involves getting their attention and interest, describing a problem or opportunity, presenting a solution or fulfillment, then giving them a chance to take action.

14 LEARN THE BASICS OF MANAGEMENT AND LEADERSHIP

Doing a job well yourself is a different challenge than managing people who are doing that work. There are people who do a certain type of work well, get promoted to managing other people who do that work, and then fail miserably as their manager or supervisor. This chapter will help you learn some basic principles of managing and leadership.

You remember that I worked for a small printing operation. On most days, if you walked into the print shop, you would've had a difficult time identifying who was the owner, the general manager, the production manager, the shop foreman, or who the individual press operators and bindery technicians were. This is because the business owners and managers worked as hard as the rest of us to produce all the printed materials we created. If there were stacks of print work that needed to be cut, folded, or shrink-wrapped, our company owners and managers didn't think it was *beneath* them to get their hands dirty or paper-cut and help get the work done.

You'll become an effective leader and manager as you get away from the idea that anyone works **for** you and always see yourself as working **with** other people. Get away from the idea that other people are at your disposal. If you want respect and dedication from your team members, you've got to give them that respect and dedication yourself.

Part of your skill development must include these management and leadership abilities. Many highly-paid business leaders may not be very talented when it comes to technology. They're not typically the ones who engineer programs or products. They're not the ones who invent valuable patents. However, these business leaders are the highest paid within any organization. Why is that?

Leaders and managers are often the highest paid because their skills are central to assembling, organizing, and directing the talents of others to accomplish major goals. You'll increase your career potential as you master basic principles of leadership and management.

Management vs. Leadership

What's the difference between leadership and management? Generally, leadership concerns itself most with **what** needs to be done, while management focuses on **how** to get it done. Leadership determines **strategy** for a group and management uses **tactics** to accomplish that strategy.

Sometimes there's no clear distinction between leadership and management. For example, a senior executive may determine the annual goals for an entire division of her company, but also take an active role in defining the smaller steps to accomplish that strategy. It's not crucial to have a tight, exclusive definition of leadership or management. Leaders will need to spend a lot of time managing, and managers will spend time leading their teams. For your purposes, understand that there are some core, basic skills needed to lead and manage other people.

Leadership and Management 101

If you asked scholars or experts which skills a successful leader or manager needs (I have asked them), you'll get a list of 10-100 skills depending on who you ask. However, out of all those skills they include in their lists, only a handful of them are what leaders and managers use every day to be successful. In other words, there are some "heavy-hitters" of effective leadership and management. The following sections represent the most fundamental skills to develop to become a successful leader or manager.

Identify and Communicate a Shared Goal or Vision

People who can unify a group to work towards a common goal or purpose make effective leaders. Leadership includes a *visionary* ability; an ability to imagine and describe an achievement not yet realized. Leaders may not know exactly how the goal will be accomplished, but they maintain an infectious enthusiasm that energizes their organizations to push for the achievement.

They communicate a mental picture that offers each contributor a personal incentive for working to accomplish the goal. When challenges or doubt surface, leaders reemphasize the vision or goal. They encourage everyone to maintain their commitment and work even harder.

This valuable leadership skill draws on other skills already discussed in this book like the ability to solve problems and the ability to persuade people. As you develop those skills, and combine them with the ability to communicate an inspiring goal, you'll be on your way to becoming an effective leader.

Challenge: Your Inspiring Vision

Answer the following questions:

- What is an inspiring goal or vision for your company or team?

- Why is it worth striving for?

- What incentive does each person have to make a significant contribution?

- *How* can your company or team accomplish it?

- What obstacles do you foresee and how can you overcome them?

A Golden Rule of Management

Managing people can be difficult because there's no set of rules to predict their behavior. Thousands of variables affect how you might manage a certain person on your team. Some of these things that may affect the way you manage people include:

- The age and/or professional experience of each person.

- Their attitudes about their work, the company, and you.

- How much pay they receive and whether they can receive additional incentives for more work.

- How their personal lives might affect their work (like health, relationships with their spouse, children, etc.)

If there are so many unpredictable variables when it comes to managing people, what set of rules could you possibly follow to effectively manage them? There are thousands of books on management skills and each one presents a different perspective. As you seek to get better work and income through developing these abilities, there's one practice that will help you become a great manager quickly:

"Don't ask anyone to do anything you're not willing to do yourself!"

This seems to be the golden rule of management, and it works magically! Most of the problems that arise from poor management have to do with some type of disrespect supervisors have for their workforce. In fact, research has shown that most people quit their jobs not because of the amount of money they get, but because of a poor relationship with their manager or supervisor.

In all my time of being managed or managing other people, I found that the idea of being *below* someone else creates resentment and kills motivation. Too often, managers feel that they are *above* the people they manage. They feel that these individuals are disposable or they're too good to do the work their employees have to do.

Observing that golden rule of management–treating people on your team as you want to be treated–will do much to ensure you're effective and respected as a manager. Not asking people to do something you're not willing to do yourself means:

- Staying late when you've asked others to work late.

- Helping with projects by doing a share of the work when deadlines approach.

- Refraining from **telling** people to do something and **asking** them to do it instead.

- Acknowledging the time, effort, and skill necessary to complete a task or project.

There are many other components of effective management like scheduling time and resources, planning, delegating, rewarding, and motivating employees. What you'll find as you work to implement the golden rule of management is that many of these other required skills mostly fall into place.

Challenge: The Best and the Worst of Managers

- Think of the *best* managers you've had. What made them effective? Why was it enjoyable to work for them? Did any of those managers observed the golden rule of management? How did they apply that rule?

- Think of the *ineffective* managers you've had. Why do you feel they were ineffective? How could they have improved?

How to Make Better Decisions

Leaders and managers have to make effective decisions. The risks and rewards of decision-making responsibility create higher pay scales for their positions. Making a decision is choosing a certain course of action when you have more than one alternative. Remember the following strategies as you work to improve your decision-making ability:

- **Slow down**. Most of the poor decisions I've seen leaders or managers make result from failing to take time and consider the results of those choices.

- **Get advice and counsel**. Everyone can offer their unique perspective on the risks and rewards of a particular decision. Knowing that you sought their input will also help generate support when the decision is made.

- **List the possible risks and rewards**. Write out the possible risks and rewards for each alternative you're faced with. Use a piece of paper, a whiteboard, or better yet, a spreadsheet you can share with others.

- **Commit to your decisions**. Being apprehensive or second-guessing a decision you made won't inspire confidence in people around you. If you want them to be excited about the course you've chosen as their leader, you've got to demonstrate confidence and enthusiasm yourself.

- **Learn quickly**. You won't know for certain, until you look back, whether a decision you made is good or bad. You should review your decisions as often as possible to determine what went right or wrong. Ask, "Which correct or incorrect assumptions did I make?" Ask, "How can I keep from making a similar mistake in the future?" Or ask, "How can I repeat this success in the future?"

Summary

- Effective leadership and management are often the highest paying career skills.

- A large part of leadership involves the ability to envision and communicate a unifying, inspiring goal for a group of people.

- Effective managers don't ask someone to do anything they're not willing to do themselves.

- As you seek to develop your leadership skills, you'll need to improve your decision-making ability. Some suggestions for making better decisions include: slow down, seek advice and counsel, list the risks and rewards of each alternative, commit to your decisions, and finally, learn quickly from your decisions whether they're good or bad.

15 LEARN HOW TO MAKE YOUR BUSINESS MORE MONEY

You'll earn even more money as you help your company make or save money. A lot of employees forget this and have a sense of entitlement for the money they're paid. If your business leader sees that you're making them more profitable through earnings or savings, they'd be dumb not to pay you more for your work.

Commissioned sales professionals fascinate me. Think what you want to about salespeople, the fact is many of them only earn income when they close a sale and actually make their business money. What do you think would happen if our hourly or salaried jobs were turned into commission-only jobs? I believe people would work a lot harder and take more initiative in their jobs.

Even though it's difficult to determine how your skills or services make or save a business money, you should understand how your contributions influence a company's profitability. You need to communicate your value in terms of profits or savings to potential employers.

Businesses can't afford to hire or give contracts to people who aren't really qualified to do the work. Businesses are interested in what you know, what you can do, and how it will help them. Even non-profit agencies and government organizations are interested in how you might make or save dollars for them.

This chapter discusses how money works and profitability. As you understand these principles, you'll be able to get better work and income by contributing more to a company's bottom line. The *bottom line* is the final calculation that determines whether a company has made a profit or lost money.

Where Does Money Come From?

In the USA, money originates from the Federal Reserve, a private financial institution. Money doesn't come from the U.S. Government as the Constitution says it should. The Federal Reserve loans it out to banks. Banks, in turn, loan it out to businesses and consumers while charging interest. The money circulates as a basis of exchange for products and services. But how do you convince a consumer or business to give you their money?

Businesses *should not focus on making money*. **You should not focus on making money**. You may argue, "Well, that's why I work. That's why businesses exist, to make money, right?" Yes, you and your business need to bring money in to operate and purchase your own necessities. What I mean is that you shouldn't focus on the income, that it shouldn't be your main goal. **Your primary concern as an employee or business owner should be to provide meaningful products and services.** Money comes as a **byproduct** of delivering those valuable products or services to other people.

Of course, you need to put a price on what you offer. Giving everything away might make you feel good about yourself, but it isn't sustainable.

Making (More) Money

The chapter on problem solving provides a good foundation for this information about understanding money. You get paid for providing solutions to problems; or satisfying an unfulfilled want or need. Here are some ideas of how you can make a business more money:

- Create a new product or service.

- Identify a new or under-served market of potential customers.

- Increase your market share for an existing product or service by offering better customer service or quality than your competition.

- Increase the profit margin for a product or service by figuring out how you can charge more for what your business offers, or reduce the cost of producing it without sacrificing quality.

Challenge: Show Them the Money

How can you make your business more money? List some ideas:

-

-

-

-

-

-

-

How to Help Companies *Save* Money

Aside from the actual cost of products companies sell, the largest expenses many companies face are for payroll and healthcare benefits. These costs keep rising. That's why when companies face hard financial times, they fire employees before they sell assets, equipment, or property.

Other expenses companies face include utilities, professional or technical services, taxes, machinery and equipment, inventory, legal fees, leases, and payments for office or warehouse mortgages, etc. You can save companies money and improve your career prospects by reducing or eliminating their dependence on these expenses. Here are a few ideas to help save your company money:

- Develop a new process for helping employees get more work done in less time.

- Create a program that automates some of the work employees normally do.

- Find ways to help employees be healthier. Many large companies are implementing wellness programs to help reduce healthcare expenses and lost productivity.

- Develop ways to manage office or warehouse space better and reduce how much is needed.

- Identify ways to legally shelter the company's taxable income and assets.

- Negotiate lower prices with suppliers or find a new supplier who charges less.

Challenge: Pinch Pennies

List some other ideas of how you could save your company money:

-

-

-

-

-

Understand Basic Financial Terms

Part of your professional development should include learning basic financial terms and concepts. Even if your job's responsibilities don't involve the company's finances, you need to know what these terms mean. They're the language that business people use to describe and monitor their companies' operations. Review the general financial terms that follow. I'm sure I've forgotten some, and there may be additional terms used frequently in your company or industry. Use your Internet searching skills to look up other financial terms that you hear about but don't understand.

Some basic financial terms to remember:

- **Revenue**: Income/earnings from business activity.

- **Profit**: The amount of gain, in dollars, after all expenses have been deducted from revenue.

- **Margin**: Amount left over from sales once production or purchase costs have been subtracted. It doesn't necessarily include other operational costs.

- **Interest**: An amount (a percentage, %) charged on borrowed money.

- **Inflation**: An increase in the amount of money in a system that leads to a rise in prices and a devaluation of money itself.

- **Appreciation**: Increase in the value of an asset.

- **Depreciation**: A reduction in the value of a financial or physical asset over time.

- **Stock**: A fractional share of the ownership of a publicly-traded company.

- **Cash-Flow**: A measure of a company's cash on-hand necessary to support its operations.

- **DOW**: The DOW Jones Industrial Average; The sum of the current stock prices of 30 major U.S. companies. This calculation attempts to reflect the general state of the economy.

- **NASDAQ**: A measurement of 3,000 companies' stock prices. It incorporates many companies within technology industries.

- **S&P**: Standard & Poor's measurement of the stock prices of 500 U.S. companies.

- **EBITA**: Earnings Before Interest, Taxes and Amortization.

- **ROI**: Return on Investment; how much was earned vs. how much was spent for a project.

- **COGS**: Cost of Goods Sold.

- **Overhead**: All incidental operating costs for a company including utilities, leases, etc. It excludes payroll and materials.

- **Capital**: Properties, equipment, or other investments capable of producing income.

- **YTD**: Year to Date; A term used in financial reports to describe financials for the current year.

- **FY**: Fiscal Year; a 12-month accounting period that may vary in its beginning and ending months. That period depends on each business or industry, not necessarily the calendar year.

Challenge: Understand a Financial Statement

Find a current financial statement for a large company. Many of them have a link called investor relations on their websites. You can find their most recent shareholder report. Once you've located one, read through the information and see how much of it you understand. Look up terms that you don't recognize. Find and study the balance sheet (usually a table or chart) that lists all the company's assets and liabilities. List some of the things you learned from reviewing the financial statement:

-
-
-
-
-
-

Develop Business Acumen

You see the term **business acumen** listed in job descriptions and resumes. What is business acumen? The Society for Human Resource Management defines it as: "Understanding certain business disciplines—for example, finance and accounting—or knowing the specific details of other functional areas in an organization like logistics or sales." Let's add to that description. Business acumen also includes:

- Being accountable for and invested in the success of other coworkers, teams, and departments as much as you are in your own.

141

- Knowing how your work and contributions can affect other operations in the business.

- Knowing how your work increases the profitability or expenses within your company.

- Identifying potential problems and bringing them to the attention of others even when those problems aren't within your area of responsibility.

- Keeping informed of changes within your industry and discovering how your company can best adapt to those changes.

- Being able to describe your company's goals, mission, and values.

- Knowing the names and roles of your organization's leadership.

Why is this knowledge and ability so important for your career? Not being aware of others' work and not caring how your work affects the company's success gives you a very poor professional reputation. I've heard people say during calls and meetings, "That's not my problem." It's like we're all sailing on a sinking ship and they refuse to help bail out water because it's not in their job description.

You might hear people call this lack of interest in others' work and responsibilities *siloing*. Siloing is defined as "information and accountability kept in isolation, in a way that hinders communication and cooperation." (*Merriam-webster.com*) Taking a wide interest in the entire company demonstrates your discipline and commitment. A disciplined and committed person is who employers want to recruit, retain, pay well, and promote.

How to Develop Business Acumen

How can you develop business acumen? Here are some strategies to start with:

- Listen closely to others as they describe anything to do with their jobs, departments, or customers.

- Find out who your competitors are and monitor how their business is going.

- Keep track of your company's customers, who they are and what challenges they face.

- Understand how government policies and legislation influence your business and industry.

- Determine if your company is currently involved in any legal proceedings, either as a plaintiff or a defendant, and try to understand why.

- Review your organization's annual budget; be able to describe the largest revenue sources as well as some of the largest expenses.

- Complete internet research or a more formal course on developing business acumen.

Summary:

- Money comes as a byproduct of delivering valuable products or services to other people and businesses.

- You can increase your chances of getting better work and income by knowing how to help companies make or save money.

- You need to understand basic financial terms and concepts.

- Developing business acumen will increase your career opportunities and it will strengthen your professional reputation.

16 LEARN NEW SOFTWARE SKILLS

If you're trying to land a job, get a promotion, or start your own business, there's probably some type of software you'll need to learn to take that next step. I know machinists who've had to learn advanced programming skills to run CNC (Computer Numerical Control) machines to stay employed. You need the ability to learn new software applications quickly to remain competitive. Fortunately, you don't need to spend a lot of money to learn many computer programs. This chapter shows how you can learn new software skills quickly on your path to better work and income.

Categories of Software and Computer Skills

Decades ago, you could hear people say things like "She's really good with computers," and "He's a computer programmer." There are so many areas and skills that have to do with computers, computer hardware, software, and networking now that it's impossible to know it all. Do any of these interest you or apply to your career goals?

- Computer programming and coding using languages like C++, Python, Apache, Java, or HTML

- Web design, development, and administration

- App development for iPhone or Android devices
- Data analysis and administration
- Operating systems (Windows, Linux, Apple iOS)
- Graphic design
- Social media
- Applied Artificial Intelligence (AI)
- Accounting software
- Cybersecurity
- Video game development
- Computer network architecture
- Software engineering
- Computer-Aided Design (CAD)
- 3D design and manufacturing
- Technical support

Should You Buy a Book?

I've bought several software books over the last decade, but they've only played a small part in the software applications I've learned to use. Software books are effective in one sense because they start out with basics like the program interface, terminology, and steps to get started. Some of these books are in-depth and show you every bit of functionality for a program.

It's been my experience that I only use about 25-50% of a software program's functionality on a regular basis. If I try to learn a new software program from A-Z, as most books approach it, I end up spending a lot of time learning and trying to remember things I'll never actually use.

I recommend learning software programs on an "as-needed" or "just-in-time" basis. Now I only use the software books I buy as references, never reading from cover to cover. If I need to learn how to set up a new payee in some accounting software, for example, I'll go to the index of the software manual and find the pages that detail how to get it done. Of course, that's only when I can't find an online tutorial first. We'll look at that option later in this chapter.

You'll find that you remember information and master software skills much better by taking this approach. Trying to learn everything about a program and then attempting to recall it when you need it is difficult and inefficient.

Install Trial or Free Versions of Software

Many software companies offer free 30-day trial installations of their software applications. When you set a goal to learn an application, just an hour a day in the trial software may be enough to develop your skills sufficiently.

An important point to remember is to only install one application per month. You can exhaust the opportunity to learn that one piece of software before the trial installation expires. The software will stop working after 30 days unless you buy the full license. If you ambitiously install the trial versions for several of these applications, then you only have 30 days to use and learn all of them. Pace yourself by taking on one at a time.

Below is a short list of software programs with free trial versions. Many of these are multimedia design applications, but others are also very useful in the business world. If there's any other software you'd like to learn, go to the manufacturer's website and see if you can use it for a free trial period. Some examples of software with free trial versions include:

- *Microsoft Word, Excel, Project, PowerPoint, etc.*

- *Salesforce.com*

- *QuickBooks Online*

- *Adobe CreativeSuite* products like *Photoshop, InDesign, AfterEffects, and Premiere*

- *Techsmith Camtasia & SnagIt*

- *JIRA* Project management

- *WIX* website creation and hosting

To find the links to download this free trial software, type in the name of the software application you want to learn into a search engine and add **"+ free trial"**. Find the manufacturer's website and locate the link to the *free trial* or *downloads* page. Installation instructions or automated wizards will help you install the software application on your computer. Some programs don't require any installation on your computer; they're web-based applications.

Challenge: Learn Software Through a Free Trial

Download one of the free trial versions of software listed above (*Photoshop* is a fun one). Then learn the basic functionality of it before the free trial period ends.

Learn Free/Open-Source Software

You can download many types of free software programs from the Internet to help sharpen your career skills and increase productivity. These software programs are entirely free, not simply for a free trial period like those we discussed in the last section. I'm not talking about games, screensavers, and other time-wasters. I mean professional-level applications that are used by businesses. You can either download and install these programs from the Internet, or use some of them as web-based programs (again, no need to install anything). Here's a short list of some free software programs I'm familiar with:

- OpenOffice Suite (openoffice.org): Free suite of programs like Microsoft Office

- MySQL (mysql.com): A database application

- SDK - Android (developer.android.com/sdk): The program used to develop mobile (Android) apps

- Apple iOS Dev Kit tools. Used to develop iPhone apps. (developer.apple.com/develop/)

- Canva (canva.com): An easy, automated tool for graphic design

- FreeCAD (freecad.org): A 3D computer-aided design tool

- Python.org (python.org/downloads/): A programming language used all over the web

- GIMP (gimp.org): A photo editing program like Photoshop

- Linux (linux.com/learn): A PC and server operating system (an alternative to Windows)

- Inkscape (inkscape.org): For vector images (like Adobe Illustrator)

- WordPress (wordpress.com): Blogging and website creation program

- GnuCash (gnucash.org): An accounting application

- Audacity (audacity.sourceforge.net): An audio editing application

- Blender 3D (blender.org): A 3D illustration program

- FreeMind (sourceforge.net/projects/freemind): A free brainstorming and creativity tool

Use the Help Menus

Just about every software application has a help menu accessible by pressing the **F1** key at the top of your keyboard, or by selecting *Help* from the menu bar. These

Help menus have search tools where you can type in words about what you're trying to do with the program. Performing a search will give you links to those topics. Some of them even link to web-based demonstrations of how to accomplish what you're trying to do. Help menus are like having your own on-call learning coach.

Challenge: Go Ahead and Press it! (F1)

Turn on your computer, open a program, and then press F1 to see what happens. Chances are, you'll open the Help menu for the current application you're using. Try it in another program that you use frequently.

Use Search Engines to Learn Software Skills

Here's another great reason to apply effective search engine skills: you can learn many types of software by searching for tutorials online. I don't believe a work week has passed in the last few years when I haven't used a search engine to find out how to do something in a software program. Here are some examples of searches I've used recently:

- *remove CSS tool tips*
- *create reflection in photoshop*
- *create named anchor wordpress page*
- *format file kindle*

Create effective searches for software tasks by including what you're trying to do and the name of the program you're using. For example:

- *format table Microsoft word*
- *create blog post wordpress*
- *remove red eye photoshop*
- *create pivot table Microsoft excel*
- *create new table mysql*
- *insert movie html 5*

Challenge: Search for a Software Tutorial

Think of a software program you use or one you'd like to learn. Next, use a search engine to locate a tutorial for a task you'd like to perform. Remember to include words that describe the task, then the name of the software application. List some keyword phrases for software tasks you'll search for:

-
-
-
-
-

View Source: A Web Design Learning Hack

If you're learning web development languages like HTML, Javascript, PHP, etc., you can view the source code for any web page displayed in an Internet browser. This shows you how other web designers and programmers create their pages. Here's how to view the source code in a few different browsers:

- *Microsoft Edge*: Press F12, then CTRL+SHIFT+G
- *FireFox*: Press CTRL+U
- *Google Chrome*: Press CTRL+U
- *Safari*: Command+Option+V (Macs)

Ask Someone

Proficient software users can demonstrate a skill more efficiently than a book or an online tutorial. You'll also get real-time feedback. If you have friends or coworkers who know a program well, just be sensitive to their time and responsibilities before you ask them to tutor you. Do all you can on your own, using some of the tools I've already mentioned. Most video call apps (*Zoom, MS Teams,*

WebEx) have screen sharing as an option. You can use this functionality to have someone demonstrate or walk you through how to do something on your computer.

Take a Paid Course

Most of the options discussed so far for learning software skills are free or inexpensive. Depending on what software you're trying to learn, or depending on your learning preferences, you may want to take a course. These usually cost money.

One advantage of taking formal software courses is that you can receive a certificate of completion. Some employers or clients may require official certification for certain programs to hire or do business with you. Most colleges have computer courses you can take. You don't necessarily have to be enrolled in a degree program to register. Some examples of other paid online courses for learning software include:

- Microsoft Certifications: microsoft.com/learning

- LinkedIn Learning: linkedin.com/learning

- Kaplan Learning: kaplan.edu

- CompTIA: certification.comptia.org

- Adobe Certifications:
  adobe.com/support/certification

- CISCO Certifications: cisco.com/web/learning

What Are Stacked Certifications?

More recruiters are placing less value on traditional college degrees when it comes to technical computer skills. They're looking at someone's certifications from software and hardware manufacturers or from institutions that offer certifications instead of degrees.

Stacked certifications, according to one of the world's leading certification organizations, are "certifications that demonstrate that you've earned multiple [progressive] certifications and have the knowledge and experience needed to grow your IT career. They validate the skills of various IT roles and show a deeper mastery, opening more job opportunities for you." (*CompTIA.org*)

It's a perfectly realistic goal to bypass traditional college degrees to focus on getting these industry certifications by themselves. Depending on your interest, goals, and again, what people will actually pay well for, investigate specific certifications you can get to earn employment in that field.

Create Your Portfolio

In some roles, I've interviewed candidates for open positions. It's an *expectation* to have a portfolio or some type of **proof of your work and capabilities**. It's not enough to just *say* that you know how to use a certain software program. Companies want actual proof of what you can do.

As you learn new software programs, collect a portfolio of work you complete. This will give job hunters or promotion seekers an advantage over others who don't have visible proof of their skills. Having a portfolio of your work or products is essential for anyone who owns their own business. Potential clients want to see a track record of your capabilities.

In my own experience, employers and clients have never asked where or how I learned my skills. They simply want assurances that I know what I'm doing. I have a large, online portfolio of work that I share to convince them I do high-quality work. We'll revisit the importance of your portfolio in the next chapter on job hunting.

Summary:

- Every job and industry require knowledge of software programs to get their work done. You need to learn new programs quickly to remain competitive.

- There are many fast and free ways to learn software programs. These include installing free trial versions, using open-source software, using the programs' Help menus, and by performing task-based searches on the Internet.

- You may need to take formal classes or training to get certified on a software program. You can find many courses online or local colleges may have the classes you want.

17 LEARN HOW TO JOB HUNT

All these skills you're learning need to result in more career marketability for yourself. You need to know how to *find* the work you're preparing for. All that effort won't amount to much if the people who are willing to pay for your abilities can't find you.

I already shared some details of my job-hunting experiences after college. It's no exaggeration to say I often spent 16 hours a day searching through job postings on the Internet. I spent so much time filling out the online applications on companies' websites but rarely got any response. My skills and their job requirements seemed to be a perfect match! Why no phone call? When I finally did get hired, an experience helped me see my job-hunting challenges in an entirely new way.

A Fortune-300 company had just hired me to develop print and computer-based training for thousands of their employees. My manager came to my team's work area a few months after I started and asked us, "Hey, we've got an open position on our team. I've been approved to hire somebody. Do you guys know anyone we can hire?" I couldn't say anything. I couldn't believe what he just asked us. I had spent so much time putting in online applications that no one apparently looked at. The company paid a large staff of recruiters, but the route this manager took to find a new-hire was to ask if we knew anyone! He didn't ask the recruiter to go search the database of resumes to see if any job seekers qualified for the position.

Now, there are many other books and resources available on interviewing, resumes, and dressing for success. These are important considerations for your job hunt and I'll leave those tactical discussions to other people. We'll discuss general job-hunting strategies. As you master new skills, you'll need to learn how to bring those abilities to the job market. I'll also share some of the painful realities you need to be aware of during your job hunt.

Packing Your Parachute

Did you receive effective career or job-hunting guidance in high school? Any in college? Teachers often repeated the advice to get good grades and go to college so you could get a good job. That advice often exhausted their job-hunting expertise. Sure, we had to complete a resume for a course or two, but anything I learned back then (not much) doesn't apply to today's job market. Do you still look through ads in newspapers or online for open positions? How many hours have you spent on job boards like *Monster.com, Careerbuilder.com* or even *Indeed.com*, the site that can search many other job sites at once? The rules have changed. You need to know what they are so you can find your next gig.

When I was unemployed, someone referred me to a book that demystified the new job market and got me on track to getting job offers. The book is Richard Bolles *What Color is Your Parachute?* It's a great guide that's updated each year. I'm not going to summarize the entire book here, but I'll list some of the points that impressed me. If you or someone you know is out of work or desperately seeking a career change, buy the book. Really. I don't recommend things for purchase that I don't really believe in.

Some of the things Bolles shared that really helped my job hunt include:

- Traditional job hunts don't work (preparing resume, submitting resume, and waiting for someone to call you).

- The route job hunters take to *find* jobs doesn't correspond to the methods recruiters use to *fill* jobs.

- Most people who land good jobs find those positions from some source other than the Internet.

- America's largest companies only employ a small percentage of the total workforce; most people work for small to mid-sized companies.

I believed most of what he wrote when I first read it, and experiences since then have further proven the truth of what Bolles taught. He said that our *first* resort for finding jobs is usually the *last* resort for people who have the power to hire someone. As soon as you complete reading this book, buy and read *What Color Is Your Parachute*. You'll find the job hunting help you need in that book.

Selling Yourself

Several months after I was hired for my first job out of college, I asked my manager what it was that convinced him to hire me. He said it was my online portfolio of work that convinced him to hire me. He knew I could do the work they needed done and had visible proof of my abilities. The samples of my work were unique enough that he knew I didn't copy them from someone else. There was one other thing that caught his interest and convinced him to hire me. I'll discuss that a little later.

You can create some portfolio items using some of the free/trial software listed in the last chapter. If it's not software, computer, or design work you do, you can show potential employers another type of proof of the work you're capable of. Take photos of something you've created or built, or give them copies of things you wrote or designed. You might write up short case studies of problems you solved for previous employers.

The point is that your resume is not enough, on its own, to market yourself. Talk is cheap! Remember that in this economy employers are very nervous about hiring someone who's not really qualified. If you can give them some type of visible proof of your abilities, they feel much more confident hiring you.

Challenge: The Elevator Pitch

How will you sell yourself to potential employers? One of the most useful job-hunting tools is the *elevator pitch*, a 30 to 60-second speech about your qualifications and what type of work you're looking for. It should be about 75-150 words long. **It should focus on how a company or potential customer can benefit from your abilities or products.** It should not focus on how much you want them to pay you, what you want them to buy, etc.

Here's an elevator pitch that a product sales rep used during his last job hunt:

> *"I enjoy matching potential customers with products and services that help their businesses grow. In the last five years, I've brought in over three-million dollars of new business to an upstart industrial supply company. For the last two years, I received top honors out of a 100-member national sales team for the largest increase in gross sales and net revenue. I can help your business find and keep new customers to increase your profits and promote growth. Would you like to know how I secured a one hundred-thousand-dollar account for my last company?"*

Do you think his elevator pitch is effective? Would you be interested in someone who had these skills and accomplishments? Why, or why not?

Now, write out and practice saying a 75 to 150-word elevator pitch to summarize **what you can offer a company**:

Eavesdropping Corporate Recruiters

I worked at a large company's headquarters in the HR department and sat right next to corporate recruiters for a few years. What I learned about how jobs are really awarded conflicts with what many job coaches advise people to do. Of course, this is how it happens at one big company, but I also gleaned some myth-debunking information from working for an even larger company before that.

One of my previous employers received over 3,000 online applications for employment each day! One mid-level I.T. position netted about 500 applications per week. That was a few years before recession, layoffs and high unemployment hit the U.S. economy. The number of applications has probably doubled by now. Some job-hunting coaches like to say hiring managers and recruiters only spend about 30 seconds scanning your resume. No, they don't. They never even look at it.

The deluge of online applications has made corporate recruiting databases unmanageable. Employment history and job skills misrepresentation is rampant. That's a nice way of saying a lot of job seekers lie about their skills and experience. Recruiters don't easily trust what many desperate, unemployed people put on paper. Even if many job applications are truthful, staffing pros have no way to personally review even a fraction of those applications. An executive recruiting manager told me their recruiting efforts are focusing on *passive recruiting*. They're going after already-employed people who haven't considered leaving their current jobs. This approach must be the reason recruiters are often nicknamed "headhunters."

One tool those recruiters do use is *LinkedIn*. Companies and independent recruiters can pay for back-end access to people's professional profiles and search for qualified candidates. If you're looking for a job, it's worth putting some real effort into your *LinkedIn* profile including job descriptions, certifications or degrees, getting recommendations from other clients or coworkers, and automating it to pull (professional) content from your blog or social media sites.

Some recruiters know very little about the nature of the jobs they're hiring for. If they knew all the technical ins-and-outs of these positions, they probably wouldn't be working as corporate recruiters. What this means is that all they have in front of them when they do an initial phone interview is a bullet-point description of the job opening. They only look at whether your application has the matching terms, phrases, degrees, and necessary experience in that field.

Your goal in the first interview is to **get them to like you**. Yes, you need to speak to those bullet-point requirements, but they can't really gauge true qualification for the job. They leave that to the hiring manager. The operative word for whether you have a good chance is when the recruiter refers to you repeatedly as being **sharp**. I gathered this from overhearing dozens of conversations between recruiters. "Yes, I liked that lady. She seemed pretty **sharp**." Or, "He was a real **sharp** guy. I think we should bring him in." So go for **sharp**. I believe *sharp* has a lot to do with your communication skills initially, then smiling, being confident and well-dressed when you show up in person.

A Few Notes on Networking and Resumes

I didn't want to make this chapter about the logistics of job hunting, but need to include a few important points. First, what role does networking play in getting hired by a company? When I was unemployed, all the push to get a network of people only generated a spreadsheet of several other unemployed people. Those who did have jobs were not usually in positions to refer me to a hiring manager. Anyone can tell you who has job openings, but to be of any real help, they need to be in an influential position to get you an interview. Recruiters who have resumes forwarded to them from friends of job seekers usually acknowledge receiving them (very politely, of course) then go back to their preferred ways of finding potential hires.

Think of networking as making professional friendships. Refer to the chapter on professional relationships for help in that area. Another important practice to adopt while you're job-hunting is **don't tell people you're looking for a job**, at least, not using those words. Tell people you are "Looking for work doing... (sales, graphic design, financial planning, programming, etc.)" Or, that you're "Looking for work as a... (customer service manager, production supervisor, etc.)" Unless people understand and remember what type of work you do, it's difficult for them to be of much help.

Remember that a resume by itself won't get you a job (see *Resumes Are Dead* by Richie Norton). The goal of your resume is to get a phone call. The object of that phone call is to get another phone call or to get an invitation to interview in person. The object of that first in-person interview is to get another one. The object of that second interview or phone call is to receive an offer, discuss salary, and determine your start date.

How and Where to Start

Realize that it's overwhelming when you try to make the giant leap from unemployment right into a new job. Your job hunt will be more effective when you can separate the process out into specific steps:

- Creating a truthful resume that's relevant to open positions; a resume that will generate phone calls from hiring managers or recruiters.

- Communicating your qualifications, being engaging and professional enough in the initial phone call to earn an invitation for an in-person interview.

- Proving during the interviews that you're capable of doing the job **and** convincing them you're enjoyable to work with.

The Stair-Step Approach to a Perfect Job

You'll have trouble going from unemployment or graduation to a perfect job. To help prevent discouragement, it's best to take a step-by-step approach leading from no job to a perfect job.

First, we must know what we're aiming for when we start a job hunt. In one episode of the television series, *I Love Lucy*, Lucy and her friend Ethel decide to go out and get jobs. They visit the *ACME Employment Agency* and meet with Mr. Snodgrass (president of the agency) for help in getting work:

Ethel: "Do you really think he can get jobs for us?"
Lucy: "Sure he can!"
Ethel: "But we don't know how to do anything!"
Lucy: "Shhhh!"
Snodgrass asks: "Well, what job did you have in mind?"
Lucy: "Uh...what kind of jobs do you have open?"
Snodgrass: "Well, what do you do?"
Lucy asks again: "What kind of jobs do you have open?"
Snodgrass asks again: "Well, what do you do?!?"

Lucy asks a third time: "What kind of jobs do you have open?"

Snodgrass: "You go first this time!"

Lucy: "Well, what do you do?"

Snodgrass: "OK. What kind of jobs do you have... NOW! NOW CUT THAT OUT! Please tell me what do you do?!? Are you stenographers?"

Lucy: "Oh yes! That's it! We're stenographers!"

Snodgrass: "Well, why didn't you say so? I have a lot of stenographic jobs available! How fast can you type?"

Lucy: "Oh...about this fast!" (She motions quickly with her fingers.)

Snodgrass: "Oh... I see. (He looks at Ethel) And how about your typing?"

Ethel: "Uh...mine's not as good as hers."

Lucy agrees: "No."

Snodgrass: "Look ladies. Let's be honest with one another. I can't find you a job until you can tell me what you can really do. Now, uh...what do you do?"

Lucy – very tentatively – asks (again): "What kind of jobs do you have open?"

Snodgrass: "Oh! Let's try it another way! I have a list. I will read off the jobs that I have available and you tell me if you've had any experience in that line."

Lucy: "Oh, fine!"

Snodgrass: "A Bookkeeper?"

Lucy and Ethel look at each other and shake their heads 'no.'

Snodgrass: "Comptometer Operator?"

Lucy and Ethel look at each other and slowly shake their heads 'no.'

Snodgrass: "Dental Technician?"

Lucy and Ethel wince their faces and shake their heads 'no.'

Snodgrass: "Insurance Adjuster?"

Lucy and Ethel give it some thought, but again indicate 'no.'

Snodgrass: "P.B.X. Operator?"

Lucy and Ethel whisper to each other discussing what

this job could be, but then finally shake their heads 'no.'
Snodgrass: "Well, I've only got one left: candy makers."
Lucy: "Oh that's it! That's our specialty!"
Snodgrass: "You're candy makers!?!"
Lucy: "Oh yes! We...we've made a lot of candy!" (As Ethel looks on in disbelief.)
Snodgrass: "Oh good. You can begin work today at Kramer's Kandy Kitchen!"
Lucy: "Oh thank you! Thank you!"

As funny as it seems, several of us have that same attitude when it comes to trying to find employment: "What kind of job do you have open?" As Lucy's experience showed, we end up getting the bottom-barrel job or no job at all. One of the most important steps for you to take is to decide exactly what type of employment you're seeking.

Let me ask you this, why do people go to college? One of the most popular answers to that question is, "So I can get a *good* job." Notice that we don't ever say, "So I can get a *perfect* job." If we expect a perfect job right out of college or after a long period of unemployment, we're just setting ourselves up for disappointment. This is one of the hard facts I've learned about job hunting. I'll share more of these **hard-but-helpful facts** with you in the summary of this chapter.

We must realize that there's a stairway to a perfect job. It helps to make clear definitions of each step we need to take towards that perfect job. First, there's *no job*, or unemployment. Then there's a *bad job*. Then there's *just a job*, followed by a *good job*, then a *great job*. Finally, there's that happily-ever-after we like to think of as the *perfect job*.

It's up to you to define each type of job category as it pertains to your own career. Making these definitions is especially important as you transition to the workforce. Just keep in mind that it's much more realistic to move from one step to the next, and difficult to get to a great or perfect job right at the beginning of your new career.

Let's walk through each step and list examples that may help you define each step in your career path.

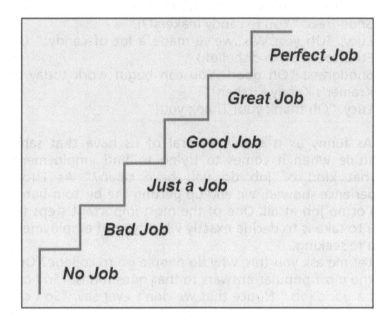

1) First, no job, or unemployment. When I was unemployed for four months after graduate school I had a rough time. Most of the difficulty came from the wrong expectations about what type of job to get. I thought my degrees entitled me to a perfect job. Unemployment may bring:

- A sense of desperation!
- Financial difficulties
- Health issues
- Low self-esteem
- Difficulty in relationships

What can you add to this list of unemployment perils? We've got lots of incentive to get employed quickly, even if the only work we can get is a *bad* job.

2) A bad job. A bad job can be better than long periods of unemployment, but not by very much! Have you ever had a bad job? I believe it's a good thing to have experienced a bad job. Bad jobs usually have:

- Poor compensation
- No health insurance
- Little opportunity for creativity
- Unhealthy working environments
- Unbearable supervisors or coworkers
- No chance for advancement
- Long hours and no vacation or paid time off
- Constant fear of being fired

As bad as all that sounds, it may be better than extended unemployment. Here's another hard-but-helpful job-hunting fact: you look much more promising as a potential employee if you currently have a job (ANY job) compared to being unemployed. Even if that job you've got right now is a bad job!

3) Just a job. When asked about their employment, have you ever heard anyone say, "It's just a job?" We might feel indifferent about out employment. It could be worse, but it could also be better. Some of the elements of having "just a job" include:

- Adequate compensation
- Some benefits and paid time off
- Reasonable working hours
- Responsibilities that you can easily handle, but they aren't very exciting or challenging
- People you work with/for who are tolerable, but perhaps not very inspiring or fun
- Few opportunities for advancement

4) A good job. Now a good job starts to look a little more desirable. A good job might include the following things:

- It pays enough to meet your needs and a little extra discretionary income
- Offers health insurance
- It has fair but not necessarily generous managers and co-workers
- It has at least a few opportunities to get promoted
- Some security and predictability
- A safe working environment
- A chance to be creative in your work

5) A great job. A great job, in your definition, might include these:

- Pay that exceeds your needs
- Health insurance
- Additional incentives for doing your job well
- A flexible schedule
- Lot of opportunities for creativity and career development
- Inspiring managers and co-workers
- A casual dress code
- No cubicles!
- A company mission that involves MORE than just making money

6) A perfect job. Our ideas of a perfect job need to be realistic. Remember that *your ideal job needs to be that intersection between what you're skilled at doing and what people will pay well for.* You'll get to define your idea of a perfect job later. A perfect job could include:

- Flexibility to work when, where, how, and if you want to

- Work that demands your interests, talents, and passions

- No dress code

- Pay that exceeds your needs and includes some type of commission structure (more work and results should equal more pay)

- Opportunities to help people live better lives

- Fun people to work with and for who help you learn and develop

Now, is it possible to jump from unemployment or college into a perfect job? What about from unemployment or college into a great job? Sure, it's possible, but not very realistic. Can you go from unemployment to a good job? That sounds a lot more reasonable. But keep in mind, you may have to go from unemployment to a bad job or a mediocre job to start building new experience and credibility. What I've shared are some of my own ideas about these different career steps. You need to define each stage for yourself!

Challenge: Your Career Path

One of the most important parts of progressing from no job to a perfect job is to define (in your own words) what each stage in your career path looks like. For example, you can list what type of compensation and benefits you expect, the type of people you work with, work schedule, opportunities for development and promotion, whether it's physical and active or sitting at a desk, etc. List some of your expectations for each one of these stages:

- **No Job**. List some of the problems associated with unemployment. *Keeping these things in mind will help you maintain motivation.*

- **A Bad Job**. List some of the elements of what you consider to be a bad job. *Sometimes a bad job is better than no job!*

- **Just a Job**. List some of the elements of a plain old job; work that's not necessarily bad, but not good either. *Remember, it's a step in the right direction!*

- **A Good Job**. List some of the elements of what you consider to be a good job. *Not quite great or perfect yet.*

- **A Great Job**. List some of the elements of a great job. *It should be about more than just money.*

- **A Perfect Job**. List some of the elements of what you consider to be a perfect job. *Remember, it has to be a job someone will pay well for. It will take time to get there, but don't give up*

Surviving Unemployment

I wrote earlier that when I finished college and moved to Denver, I thought I'd have a great job within a few weeks. I had solid work experience accrued throughout my college years and a respectable degree in my pocket. But those two weeks turned into four full months before I landed a job in the training industry.

Those four months without work took a terrible toll. I didn't sleep soundly for more than a few hours each night. Stress and worry tear down immunity quickly. I got so sick with the flu that looking back, I think I could have died. The few thousand dollars we had saved evaporated quickly and my wife was pregnant with our first child; no health insurance!

I spent most of each day either searching Internet job sites or driving around commercial areas in Denver inquiring at businesses about openings. I annoyed friends and family members with my attempted networking. Worst of all, I lost hope and let my self-esteem deteriorate. Here are some important lessons I learned about how to survive unemployment:

- **Job Hunt 2-4 Hours Per Day**. After a few hours of searching new listings on job sites each day, each additional hour I spent became more ineffective. I would read the same postings over and over again. I would check for email messages from people in my network dozens of times each hour. While all those things need to be done each day, they only deserve a few hours of attention. I also found that Monday mornings and Friday afternoons are useless times for trying to contact people. Use those times to do something else.

- **Get a Part-Time Job and a Mobile Phone with a PROFESSIONAL Email Address**. I worried incessantly about missing a recruiter's phone call or email if I left my perch by the phone and computer. I thought I couldn't afford a cell phone with a data plan. A smart phone would have permitted me to get out of the house much more than I did without missing a job-related call or message. I could have easily worked a part-time job in the afternoons or evenings to slow our financial drain. The activity would have distracted me from the worries and concerns of unemployment. It may have provided some much-needed socialization and could have even led to a more permanent career. If your email is something funny or risky, get a new one for your job hunt and to put on your resume.

- **Learn New Skills.** Knowing that my job hunt was leaning more and more towards instructional design work, I should have spent an hour each day learning new software without having to spend any money on it. (Refer back to the chapter on learning software skills.) I could have added the results of this software study to my online portfolio for better career marketability.

- **Exercise.** Even a mild amount of activity would have done so much to reduce physical and psychological stress. The exercise would have cleared my mind and enabled me to concentrate better. That ability to focus would have come in handy during the countless resume revision sessions.

- **Pursue Hobbies.** At my wife's insistence, I attended an amateur radio (HAM) certification workshop while I was unemployed. She wanted me out of the apartment! I went to the classes, took the test, and received my license. For some reason, I added that HAM radio license to the certifications section of my resume. I mentioned earlier that when I did get hired, and asked my boss what it was that convinced him to hire me, he said there were two specific things. The first was the online portfolio of my work. The second? He said he hired me because I had a HAM radio license! He was familiar with the technical nature of getting an FCC license and thought that if I could pass that, then I should have no problem working on his technical training team. So, take time when you're unemployed to pursue some hobbies. It will help you deal with stress more effectively and may also be the gateway to a new job or career.

- **Have Fun.** I knew that I would eventually get a job, but I let fear and anxiety ruin what could have been an enjoyable four-month semi-vacation. I could have read more books on my to-read list or gone on longer walks with my wife. I should have taken many more naps. I regret that so much of that time was spent in fruitless searching and worrying.

ALWAYS Look for Your Next Job

This doesn't mean secretly searching job listings and interviewing while on your current employer's time and payroll. Always looking for your next job means no matter how happy and secure you feel in your current position, you should always look for and chase better opportunities within or outside of your current organization. It means continually adding new accomplishments and responsibilities to your resume. It includes cultivating professional relationships using the approaches we discussed in that earlier chapter.

You can't afford to quit your job to devote time to education, can you? How can you maintain your full-time employment and still learn things to advance your career? You can do both at the same time! Here are some ways you can learn on-the-job:

- **Get yourself a mentor, maybe two.** You'll learn career skills much more effectively when you have someone who helps teach and motivate you. Mentors can demonstrate skills and share information not available in textbooks. How do you get a mentor? Find someone who has the knowledge, skill, and experience you want and ask for coaching and feedback. Sure, some insecure people won't agree to this because they see your ambition as a threat. In most situations, you'll compliment potential mentors with your request. They'll often make time to help you.

- **Volunteer for challenging projects**. When my director said our company needed training videos created for a safety program and new hire orientation, I volunteered to produce them. The projects encompassed enormous amounts of work and coordination, but I learned video production from start to finish. The company essentially paid me to learn this new skill. Do you have opportunities at work to volunteer for new projects? Step up to those projects that offer opportunities to learn something new. Be careful of seeking projects that increase your workload without learning opportunities.

- **Keep a work or project journal**. You take notes in school or training, what about at work? I know several people who keep "little black books" of notes and hacks for getting things done. My older brother is a professional sound engineer and he uses these "sidekicks" frequently. He'd probably sacrifice a limb before parting with these notes. Did you make a mistake on a project that ended up costing time and money? Write down what you learned as a hedge against it happening again. Have you discovered an efficient shortcut to being more productive? Take notes so you remember to use it next time.

- **Bring a book**. At first, I worried when my managers saw design, programming, or project management books open on my desk. They didn't seem to mind, so I worked through a chapter each day and incorporated what I learned into current projects. Businesses and employees both benefit in an atmosphere that encourages learning and improvement.

- **Ask!** Absorb as much as possible in your work environment by asking everyone questions about what they do. Don't tax their time expecting in-depth explanations. Ask them to define a term you haven't heard before. Invite them to diagram a process for you. Ask them how they got to where they are in their careers. Making this informal learning a habit will give you a broad grasp of the company and build your highly-marketable business acumen.

- **Keep things up-to-date**. Always add accomplishments from your current job to your resume. Be sure to keep your professional profile (LinkedIn) current and ask for recommendations from past coworkers and managers. It's very helpful, as you advance in your career, to keep an employment log with exact job titles, managers' names, start and stop dates, and addresses for your employers. It makes job applications go much smoother in the future when you have this information in one place.

How to Overcome Underemployment

What is underemployment? If you're underemployed, it means you've got a job, but the job's responsibilities and demands offer no challenge to your interests or abilities. When you're underemployed, you're probably not being paid as much as you're worth either. Underemployment in the workforce is as much of a drag on the economy as unemployment is. Here are some symptoms of underemployment:

- Boredom and inability to concentrate

- Trying to get out of projects rather than taking them on

- You have a larger workload than coworkers who are in the same job and salary range

- You feel that if you were suddenly fired, that wouldn't be such a bad thing

How do you overcome underemployment? For starters, don't just *read* this book. **Apply** what you read and learn. Aside from that, have an honest discussion with your manager and express your feelings. Seek a promotion or another opportunity in other departments.

You can overcome underemployment by simply quitting your job. Pursue an entirely new career path. After four years in one position at a company, with no other opportunities immediately available, I quit because I felt so professionally stagnant. True, I had some freelance work lined up before I left, but the courage to jump ship sparked a new fire of motivation and ambition for me.

How to Get a Raise

Everyone wants a raise. Do you? What do you have to do to qualify for and receive a larger paycheck? While no formula is foolproof, you can eliminate most of the guesswork by remembering three important keys:

- **Deserve a raise**. You've got to be doing more than what you were first hired to do. Tenure with an employer doesn't provide a good argument for deserving more money. The work you do must increase the company's bottom line or significantly reduce expenses if you hope to get more money for doing it.

Now is a great time to define and calculate how your work increases profitability. Commissioned and incentive-based positions get a direct percentage or bonus based on measurable results. The rest of us have to somehow calculate if we're really worth more dollars to our employers or not.

- **Demonstrate that you deserve a raise.** You'll have to make a case to your boss that you deserve the raise. Show those numbers that prove the company's making or saving more money because of your work. Show the dollar amounts from invoices, accounts, and ledgers. Estimates won't convince your boss or the payroll folks.

  You may not have access to those dollar amounts. You'll have to build your case based on increased work responsibilities since you were first hired. Try to find the job description for your position when first started your job. Show how what you do now exceeds the original job description and expectations.

  Perhaps you've learned new technical skills on your own time that benefit the business. You may routinely mentor and coach others on your team. You may have chosen to do projects on your own that were traditionally outsourced. Before your boss or company will pay you more, you must demonstrate that you're doing more.

- **Ask for a Raise!** A tough economy invites a strong-armed approach. A signed offer for more money at another company works wonders when trying to negotiate a new salary at your current employer. Your company's got to be in a financial position to give you a raise if you expect to have any real leverage. Raises must usually be approved by someone higher than your immediate supervisor. It's more difficult when your position is capped within a certain salary range. Some great resources for comparison of your salary are available at *Payscale.com* or *Salary.com*.

Summary: Hard But Helpful Job-Hunting Facts

Let me end the chapter with this: there's more to your employment than just making a living. The world's got problems and needs your unique abilities to make it a better place. Understand that you have some part to play in this world. As you commit to finding and fulfilling your mission in life, your time spent learning new skills will be a great investment. As you make your unique contributions, doors will open for you to get a good job and perhaps a perfect job. The following points may be hard to accept, but they're useful to remember during your job hunt:

- There's really one main purpose or goal for a resume: simply to get a phone call. A resume will not get you a job. Remember, its main purpose is to get you a phone call. The purpose of the first phone call is not to get a job, it's to get an appointment for an interview. That first interview's purpose isn't to get a job offer…it's to get you a second interview. THEN the purpose of that second interview is to get them to call you and extend the job offer.

- Your first interview in mid-to-large companies is usually with a recruiter or human resources rep who may not know much about the actual job responsibilities. You want to make a good enough impression on them that they set up an interview with the hiring manager.

- Most of what people learned to do their current job successfully didn't come from school or formal training. It came from learning on-the-job or through real-world experience. The most important thing you'll take from your formal education or training is learning how to learn!

- You can save a lot of time and get an advantage over other job seekers if you read and apply information from Richard Bolles' book, *What Color is Your Parachute?* There are all sorts of ideas and strategies about how to find a job. After studying many of them, the most valuable job-hunting approach I learned about is in that book. I recommend you buy it and take notes on what you learn. It will make the time you spend job hunting much more effective.

- The rule used to be to plan on about one month of job searching for every $10K of annual salary you expected. For example, plan on job hunting three months for a $30K/year job. When unemployment is high in a tough economy, you probably need to double that. Depending on your experience and skills, prepare for at least three months of searching for a $30K/year job and possibly longer for higher salaries.

- It's realistic to accept a bad or mediocre job after unemployment or right out of college to build experience.

- You are much more attractive as a potential employee if you are currently working (even in an unrelated job) than if you have no job at all.

- Large corporations sometimes receive up to 10,000 online applications per day! Unless your resume/application is 99.9% relevant to the job description, no one will look at your resume. According to what some recruiters say, the number of online job applications has tripled over the last few years. It's come to a point where they don't even trust much of the information people put in their online job applications because desperate people misrepresent their skills and work experience.

- Many companies are searching or paying others to research potential employees' social media profiles. Are your *LinkedIn*, *Facebook*, and *Twitter(X)* accounts professional? Make sure to limit the visibility of or delete items that may hurt your chances for getting hired.

- Generally, companies will not pay moving expenses for positions lower than management or for people right out of college. That is, unless you're an engineer, programmer, scientist, MBA graduate, or in medical professions. Unfortunately, recruiters may rule you out just based on where you live without even looking at your qualifications.

18 LEARNING TO THINK
FOR YOURSELF

I mentioned before that I spent a hot summer day in the Southwestern sunshine painting a house to earn money. My dad watched as I unloaded all the painting equipment from my trailer. He said, "You know, God gave you a brain so you wouldn't have to sweat so much."

I really didn't like what he said, but the truth of the statement haunted me for months. It wasn't too long after that when I started taking classes, buying books, and teaching myself higher paying skills. I eventually got higher paying work, which required a lot less physical effort. Yet even when I had a series of good jobs there was still much about them that I didn't enjoy. My definition of better work and income evolved to mean starting my own business. So, I did the research, took the risks, and learned what I needed to do to start my own venture.

I see a lot of people around me who work very hard, but who still don't receive enough income to live very comfortably. This doesn't seem fair or just, but that's the way things are. Rather than wasting time trying to blame someone else, the government, or some organization for these problems, we should focus our energy to adapt and thrive regardless of the circumstances. We've got to **combine our hard work with smart work**.

Perhaps many of the economic struggles people face come from trying to play a new game by the old rules. Schools and government agencies publish lists of what the good jobs are or what the most promising careers might be. Yet many people who've taken those career paths are stuck in dead-end jobs or they're out of work altogether. Some careers and businesses that pay well *now* may be extinct in a year or two.

While growing up, if I had some type of problem and asked my dad about it, expecting some type of answer from him about how to solve my problem, he'd ask, "Well, what do **you** think?" I felt frustrated when he responded like this, but as I've gotten older, I realized Dad wasn't trying to avoid helping me. He did more for me than parents who try to solve their kids' problems for them. He wanted me to learn to think for myself. That ability has turned out to be a great gift and presented many opportunities.

The most important ability you can develop to ensure ongoing professional success and the best income is adaptability; to learn new skills quickly. You can't expect academic or government programs to keep pace in providing relevant education as fast as business and technology change. **Part of developing that adaptability includes learning to think for yourself.**

What is Thinking for Yourself?

Thinking for yourself means you make conscious decisions about what you learn and believe. Thinking for yourself means that you can set aside fears, prejudice, bias, social pressure, and even disregard authority in some instances to come to your own conclusions. Initially, people who think for themselves are often mocked, discounted, abandoned by their peers, or fired from their jobs because they don't readily accept what other people tell them to do and to believe. We've all experienced some of this in some degree. And I think we're all guilty for discounting people who listened to the beat of a different drummer.

Sometimes we call people who think for themselves innovators, the people who introduce new ideas or concepts. We give them that honored label if what they introduce doesn't make us too uncomfortable or challenge what we think we already know. Can you recall any famous historical figures or innovators who **didn't** think for themselves? Whoever succeeded by following someone else's beliefs? Here are a few examples of people who thought for themselves:

- **Albert Einstein** was very suspicious of educational authority and learned to trust his own curiosity. He often skipped class to study things that were outside the curriculum of his school work, and often ditched lectures because he felt professors weren't teaching him anything new. As a result of Einstein's determination to think for himself, the world has benefited from his work on relativity, energy, and quantum mechanics. There's a little more on his learning strategies at the end of this chapter.

- **Joan of Arc** learned to think for herself. She defied tradition, followed her own convictions, and led the French to important victories over the invading British armies in the early 1400s. Women serving in military leadership positions was unheard of in her time. As *Biography.com* describes Joan of Arc, she demonstrated "a reliance on individual experience, as opposed to that found through the institutions of the church." Joan d'Arc's fierce independence still serves as a great inspiration to people hundreds of years after she died. Yes, she was killed for what she did, but she achieved immortality.

- **Rosa Parks** also demonstrated great courage and showed us what it means to think for yourself. She deliberately broke discriminatory, racist laws when she refused to yield her bus seat to another passenger. After being arrested, her experience launched a boycott of public transportation and the effort finally led to nationwide repeals of unfair, prejudiced segregation policies. Rosa Parks' intellectual independence and courage gave the civil rights movement in the United States much-needed momentum.

- **Steve Jobs** showed he valued thinking for himself when he left college to educate himself and start *Apple Computer*. He's credited with many innovations and has changed the way the world communicates with the introduction of the iPhone. If you read more about Steve Jobs, you'll see that he made a lifelong habit of disregarding conventions and designed new products to better solve peoples' problems.

These are all famous people who learned to think for themselves. There are people around us who know how to think for themselves and live better lives because of it.

For example, a close friend of mine worked as a machinist for several years and eventually realized he knew more about running the company than the guys who owned the business, but the owners kept most of the money he made for the company. This friend of mine learned what he needed to know to start his own company. He quit his job, financed some equipment, and has made millions of dollars running his own business. Many successful entrepreneurs are people who've learned to think for themselves.

And while we're talking about entrepreneurs and people who think for themselves, another one bought a pile of books about starting her own business and now owns a multi-million-dollar cleaning services company. People told her she couldn't do it. She had a family to take care of, no college degree, and lacked the self-confidence she wanted. But she knew she could think for herself and figure out how to start and maintain a successful company.

As these friends learned, there are way too many people who want you to accept their doubts and disbelief. If you learn to think for yourself and follow your own convictions, you can live a wonderful, successful life.

Challenge: Other Examples of Independent Thinkers

Many of the significant achievements in the world come from people who think for themselves. I mentioned Albert Einstein, Joan of Arc, Rosa Parks, and Steve Jobs as a few examples. Who else can you think of that made major changes in the world because they were independent thinkers?

What Thinking for Yourself Is Not

Thinking for yourself doesn't mean you should discount or entirely dismiss anything that anyone else says. You can listen to and consider what other people have to say, and evaluate the credibility of what they share before you decide to accept or believe it yourself. Thinking for yourself doesn't mean being stubborn or obstinate just for the sake of being independent. Thinking for yourself doesn't mean you should distrust everything someone else says or writes. In your quest to become an independent thinker, you'll have to learn how to identify what sources of information are trustworthy.

Thinking for yourself doesn't mean you have to reinvent the wheel for everything you learn. You don't have to reproduce all the research and discoveries other people have made throughout history to know and understand them for yourself. Understand that thinking for yourself doesn't mean you refuse to learn from other people. Learning from them is a critical piece of your professional development. You just need to go about it the right way so that you're not misinformed or deceived. Let's look at a few examples of people who don't really grasp what it means to think for yourself.

- Jason was a know-it-all if there ever was one. He thought he knew more than everyone else and wouldn't listen to or learn from them. He didn't realize that being arrogant and unteachable is not the same as thinking for yourself. Our industry was changing quickly. On a few occasions, I suggested that if he didn't learn a specific type of software, he'd be in danger of losing his job. The work he'd been paid for in the past was becoming obsolete. He was overconfident and eventually lost his job. His responsibilities were absorbed by some other people on our team and the company hired someone with a more up-to-date skillset than Jason.

- A manager believed that thinking for herself and being innovative meant putting a lot of time and money into a project her director didn't know about. She spent $30K developing some online and printed training resources that didn't align with what company leadership wanted and that money ended up being wasted. She didn't get fired, but her director took away her ability to spend any budget money and certainly didn't trust her for more important projects in the future.

Thinking for yourself doesn't mean being stubborn, arrogant, and unteachable. Thinking for yourself *does* include respecting, listening to, and learning from other people. You accept the truth of what others say, and politely disregard or forget their subjective opinions and misinformation. You persist in the direction of your own convictions but appreciate that others have different perspectives than you do.

Benefits of Thinking for Yourself

Do you ever feel like other people have too much influence over your life, or the way you think? How would your professional and social lives be different if you developed a lot more self-assurance?

As you learn to think more independently, you'll feel more self-confident. Feeling more confident helps you communicate more clearly. It helps you focus on your goals and achieve more. Being more confident in yourself makes you more attractive to other people. You'll find more innovative solutions to problems. This makes you more valuable to employers. The more valued you are as an employee or entrepreneur, the more money people are willing to pay you.

There are even more benefits from learning to think for yourself more often. When you improve your independent thinking, you can break away from the crowd mentality and dismiss a lot of the propaganda that surrounds us. How many people succeeded in life because they did what everyone else does? Do you think you can really be extraordinary by following the crowd? **The crowd doesn't want you to distinguish yourself.** They want you to be mediocre, like they are. Every news source has some bias or agenda they want you to believe. In truth, most people believe your commitment to think for yourself is a threat to their own identity. Caring too much about what other people think of you will forfeit your dreams and goals in life. Thinking for yourself will keep other peoples' opinions from sabotaging your destiny.

That leads to another benefit of learning to think for yourself. As you develop this skill, you'll be able to identify and resist forms of persuasion other people try to use on you. Have you ever been talked into buying something you didn't want? Did someone trick you into attending an event you didn't really want to go to? Or maybe someone talked you into getting a tattoo that you wish could just disappear. Whatever the situation was, did you think about how these people persuaded you to do it? Wouldn't you like the knowledge and confidence to resist these people in the future? Thinking for yourself will give you that power. There's more on resisting manipulation in a few pages.

Consider the consequences of not thinking for yourself. These might include feeling like your life is controlled by someone else. Failing to think for yourself will erase any sense of self-confidence you have. Letting other people determine your ideas and opinions makes your life boring and predictable. Not thinking for yourself makes you feel like you're just a program, a robot, a product of your environment or circumstances.

As you stay committed to this path and learn specific ways to improve your independent thinking, keep all these benefits of thinking for yourself in mind. And remember the consequences of letting others do your thinking for you.

Challenge: Rewards for Independent Thinking

We already listed more self-confidence, a better ability to solve problems, distinguishing yourself from the crowd, and increased ability to resist manipulation. As you become a more independent thinker, how will your life and career improve? List some personal benefits you can get from improving your ability to think for yourself:

-
-
-
-

What will happen to your hopes and dreams if you only listen to what everyone else tells you to do? What will happen if you care too much about what others think?

List some of the consequences you'll face if you DO NOT become an independent thinker:

-

-

-

-

HOW to Think for Yourself

People *speak* highly about independent thinking. How many times have you heard the phrase, "Think outside the box" when people describe themselves or others? Yet most leaders, governments, teachers, and managers want you to think safely within the limits of their own ideas. It's time to quit subjecting our mind power to others. How do you do it? In the next few pages, let's look at some suggestions to help you think more independently.

First, Assume Nothing

An assumption is information or an idea that's taken for granted. An assumption is something you already *think* you know or accept to be true. We need to assume some things in life, but assuming can also trap us in self-defeating thought patterns. If there's a problem that you're working to overcome without making progress, you may be working with incorrect assumptions.

- How might your life improve by reconsidering your own assumptions?

- Which assumptions about your education, employment, business, or the economy might be trapping you?

- How do you identify and replace incorrect assumptions?

Develop Your Imagination

Imagination serves you much better than memorization will. Considering *what may be* might prove to be more profitable than *what has been*. Acting on faith means pressing forward to realize things you haven't seen before.

"When you keep doing what you're doing, you'll keep getting what you're getting!" To paraphrase Einstein, "You can't solve problems using the same kind of thinking you used to create them." And Robert Pirsig wrote, "If a factory is torn down, but the rationality which produced it is left standing, then that rationality will simply produce another factory" (from *Zen and the Art of Motorcycle Maintenance*). Your professional success will depend on your ability to develop imaginative, innovative thinking.

Here are three ways to improve your imagination:

- **Read More Fiction**. Fiction doesn't mean untrue. Best-selling author Orson Scott Card defended (Science) Fiction as "what may be." Many dismissed George Orwell's 1984 as unrealistic back when he wrote it. Yet many of his imaginative elements exist today; cameras and monitors everywhere, rewriting news, and redefining words to manipulate people. You can expand and strengthen your imagination by "visiting" the imaginary worlds others have invented. Reading more fiction will open your mind to new possibilities and creative opportunities

- **Ask More Questions**. Why? The earlier chapter on problem solving discussed question-asking in context of identifying solutions. Here it's mentioned again as a tool to expand your imagination and creativity. One question that's particularly effective at expanding your imagination is, "What if?" and another is, "Why not?" Asking questions is a humble invitation to learn and grow. Asking questions prompts you to consider new possibilities. You're more likely to overstep the status quo. Progress comes slowly, if at all, by rehashing what we already know. Progress comes when we stretch our minds beyond old patterns of thinking.

- **Improvise and Create More Stories**. Narratives don't have to be extraordinary or fantastic to be effective. When you communicate try to illustrate your point with a story. This ability to produce concrete examples to communicate your point is a growing trend in leadership development. Just like exercising a muscle, forcing yourself to improvise more stories will expand your imagination and creativity. This skill will prove to be a milestone in your professional success.

Distrust Social Proof

As you improve your ability to think for yourself, one major threat is what's known as "social proof." One source defines social proof as, **"a psychological phenomenon where people assume the actions of others in an attempt to reflect correct or acceptable behavior for a given situation."** (from the not-so- authoritative, socially-created *Wikipedia.org*)

We can define social proof as a "herd mentality." People who rely on social proof believe that they're safe doing what everyone else appears to be doing. You even see people who market products or programs online using phrases like "10,000 people can't be wrong!" But that many people and millions more CAN be wrong about something. At one point, just about everyone in the world believed the world was flat, and that the sun orbited the earth, but just because millions believed this didn't make those ideas true. (Even though some movements to disassociate people's thinking from reality have renewed the idea of a flat earth!) **If enough people believe something, that doesn't make it true.**

You see all sorts of examples when people try to manipulate the power of social proof for their own advantage. For instance, research has shown that a significant percentage of the so-called followers or friends on celebrities' or political figures' social media profiles are fake accounts. I suspect these people pay agencies to get thousands if not millions of these fake friends and followers so it appears they are more popular than they really are.

Many people are paid by manufacturers to leave positive product reviews on sites like *Amazon.com*, even if they never purchased or used the product. These tactics are deceptions and they hope to bypass your critical thinking ability. They want you to believe what they say or buy what they're selling, based on social proof.

You'll also see social proof being manipulated in the form of comments on social media posts and news stories or blog posts. This deception isn't always in the form of positive reviews or comments. People post ignorant or biased comments under a fake identity to make anyone who doesn't agree with their ideas appear foolish or misinformed. Owners of a review site falsified poor reviews for movies or producers who didn't agree with their political agendas.

These are examples of how social proof isn't trustworthy. You see why basing your beliefs and decisions on social proof is very damaging. You understand social proof can be a road block to your commitment to think for yourself. As you work to become more independent in your thinking, you've got to insulate yourself from these fallacies.

First, think of all the areas in your life where social proof might be influencing you. It might be through your social media accounts. You might spend a lot of time reading through comments on news sites or blogs and that may be influencing you more than you want to admit. Think of the friends or the co-workers you interact with. How do those people influence what you do with your time? Consider the traditions you've inherited from the family you grew up with, like political inclinations, socioeconomic bias, or religious views.

I'm not suggesting you abandon all these things just for the sake of being intellectually independent. Be aware of what these influences are and how they might affect your life for better or worse. Here are a few other strategies for avoiding that herd mentality; how you can keep it from overriding your own reason and judgment:

- **Despise groupthink.** *Groupthink* is the practice of thinking or making decisions as a group in a way that discourages creativity or individual responsibility. (*Merriam-Webster.com*) Do an internet search for examples of groupthink to learn what it is and how to avoid it.

- You can lessen the herd's influence on your thinking by **limiting the time you spend on social media sites.** People think these sites and apps are free. They make money from advertisers, campaigns, and government bureaus who want to shape your beliefs about products, candidates, and behaviors. Be very wary of what you see in your feeds. Algorithms shape those messages to reflect agendas of their owners and advertisers.

- Remember that just because a book is bestselling, that doesn't mean it's really one of the best books. **To think outside the box, you must read outside the box.** Ask people you know and respect for reading recommendations.

- **Make decisions based on evidence and facts.** Do your own fact finding and checking. Although not foolproof, your intuition will serve you much better than other social influences.

- You may get your news from a source that's socially or politically biased. Decide to read and **get your information from a more objective source.** (And let me know if you can find one!)

- Are you following someone on a social media site who has lots of followers and friends, but posts information you know is narrow-minded and unreasonable? You can **hide, unfriend, or unfollow those people to minimize their influence on you.**

- Perhaps certain friends talk you into spending too much time in some worthless activity, talk you into drinking too much, or they're prejudiced against one group or another. **Spend less time with these people** to reduce or eliminate their influence on your thinking and decisions.

- You can also reduce the effect of social proof on your purchasing decisions by learning **to identify product reviews from paid or biased sources.** Sometimes those reviews come from people who are friends and family members of the company selling it. There's really no key to deciphering real from fake product reviews. Read them and see if the review is giving specific, balanced information about the product or company. Remember that there are competitors who will leave hateful, misinformed reviews about a company on review sites to hurt their competition.

Realize that simply admitting what sources of social influence are around you is an important step in becoming a more independent thinker. One more important point when it comes to social proof: the earlier examples show that just because many people believe or do something, it doesn't make it the right thing to do. There's a counterpoint to this. **Just because a lot of people DO believe something, it doesn't necessarily make that thing *incorrect*.** Don't dismiss what's right just for the sake of being different. Don't let the crowd make those decisions for you about *anything*, whether they're wrong **OR** right.

Challenge: Disproving Social Proof
Answer these questions:

- How is social influence affecting your thought processes and beliefs?

- In addition to the strategies already mentioned, how can you reduce the harmful effects of social proof and peer pressure in your life?

Keep Fear from Hijacking Your Thinking Process
Another major obstacle to thinking for yourself is fear! Fear is the expectation of something bad or unpleasant. Another definition of fear is an unpleasant emotion caused by being aware of danger. The danger we sense that creates the feeling of fear **can be entirely *imaginary*.** It doesn't have to be a *real* threat which puts our mind and body into a fight, flight, freeze, or flock response. How does fear affect our brain function and our ability to think rationally? Let's consider some anatomy and physiology to answer that question.

The outer region of the brain is the cerebral cortex. It's responsible for complex thinking, analysis, language, and navigation. This is the part of our brain that ***we wish was in control all the time***. We'd make better decisions and live happier lives if the cerebral cortex called all the shots.

An area in the center of our brain is the limbic cortex, and more specifically, the amygdala. Some biologists call this area our "lizard brain" because it seems to function like an animal's survival instinct, taking over control of our body when a threat is present *or perceived*.

The survival function of this inner brain region causes what's known as an amygdala hijack. The amygdala bypasses the outer, rational part of our brain and essentially tells it to be quiet. The lizard brain says, "Shut up you outer, rational thinking part of my brain! I'm taking over to save this dude!" Hormones are injected by the hypothalamus into the bloodstream, adrenaline mainly, which increases the heart rate, dilates the pupils, and increases blood sugar metabolism to prepare the body to run from or fight the perceived threat it fears.

That's a very simplified explanation of what happens in our brain and bloodstream when we become afraid and sense a threat. But how does fear and this type of cognitive response affect our ability to think for ourselves? Again, if we perceive a real or imaginary threat, the amygdala and hypothalamus take over and shut down the parts of our brain that are responsible for complex, critical thinking. If these functions in our brains are shut down, then we're at the mercy of our emotions and survival instincts. We may do or say things that we regret or make us feel embarrassed.

Some people and organizations deliberately manipulate our fears to override our intellectual independence. Can you think of any example right off? Politicians and political parties often create a sense of fear in people and insist the only way to avoid the danger or perceived threat is to sign their petition, give them your vote, take their pill, or contribute to their campaigns. Many religious groups do the same thing; describing judgments and retribution which will come for not adopting their beliefs and way of life. Activists from one group or another also base their campaigns on fear. The strategy is called *alarmism* or *catastrophizing*. It's a form of manipulation. They work to get people agitated, unreasonable, and vulnerable to someone else's control.

Many people in these groups don't want you to think for yourself. They want to stimulate that fight or flight response and get you to believe or do what they've determined you should do. They don't want your outer cortex of rational thinking to look at problems logically. Manipulative people want to keep you subjected to them through arousing your fears and controlling you through that irrationality.

Again, if you allow other people to make you afraid, you'll essentially surrender your own thinking and decision-making powers. People will take advantage of you and keep you from realizing your true potential. As you learn to recognize when fear hijacks your rational thinking, you can take steps to reclaim it. You'll improve your ability to think for yourself regardless of fear. So how do we keep fear from overtaking our independent, rational thinking?

Keep Fear Out of the Equation

First, stay on the alert when people try to generate a sense of fear in you. It might be the first step in attempting to control you and your beliefs. Be suspicious of anyone, any agency, organization, or news story that **first tries to make you afraid of something.** Recognize this fear mongering as an attempt to get your survival-motivated amygdala to control you, not the rational, independent part of your brain. **Simply recognizing these attempts is the most important method to disarm fears.**

Another strategy for keeping fear from hijacking your thinking is to do what Dale Carnegie suggested. He said you can resign yourself to the worst thing that could happen, imagine it already DID happen, and then try to improve the situation. For example, if you're afraid of losing your job and that fear is keeping you from thinking logically about your circumstances, then just accept the fact that you'll be fired and then decide what your next steps should be. This is a very effective way to keep fear from sabotaging your logical, independent thinking. If you want to learn more about this strategy, read Dale Carnegie's book, *How to Stop Worrying and Start Living*.

Challenge: Bring Fears into Perspective

Visit a few online news sites and identify headlines of articles that try to activate fear. Then read through the articles themselves and see if the facts of the story are as bad as the headline makes it appear.

Next, list what fears are keeping you from thinking for yourself and then determine what you can do to dismiss those fears. Then answer the following questions:

- What people and organizations try to make you afraid and surrender your independent thinking?

- How can you keep them from controlling your thinking by making you afraid?

Learn to Identify and Resist Forms of Manipulation

What you learned earlier about persuading people will also help you learn to recognize forms of manipulation when people attempt to use them on you. As you improve your ability to think more independently, an important step will be to recognize and resist forms of manipulation.

There's no shortage of books, blogs, articles, and courses out there that claim to teach you how to get people to do what you want. People spend millions of dollars learning from psychologists and sales trainers how to get other people to do something. Internet marketers practice all kinds of tricks to take your money in exchange for a poor but hyper-marketed product. In too many cases we're left poorer, disappointed, and wonder how they convinced us to make a purchase we regret so much.

You need to recognize these techniques so you can neutralize them and improve your independent thinking. Remember the differences: that persuasion is communication meant to influence people to believe or do something *willingly*. It's presenting someone with reasons and incentives for taking action. **Getting people to do something if they are unwilling or resentful is not persuasion—that's called** *compulsion* **or** *manipulation*. To repeat the definition from the earlier chapter, manipulation is defined as, "controlling by artful, unfair, or insidious means especially to one's own advantage."

People the world over and from every walk of life try to manipulate our desires to gain something good or to avoid something bad. It's not just for making purchases, but also for getting you to sign a petition, to vote the way they want us to, to give them money, time, etc.

How can you resist manipulation and not get pulled into doing or believing something you don't want to? **Recognizing when one of these tricks is being used on you usually disarms it right away.** For example, a few years ago my wife and I were shopping to buy a new car. I had studied persuasive (sometimes manipulative) techniques in my graduate program and was employed at that point creating training programs for a large group of sales agents. I was a little savvy to how salespeople try to get our money from us.

We went to a car dealership to look at a specific car. We'd already done a lot of research and determined what model we wanted and how much we could afford to pay. The sales guy we sat down with realized he didn't have to sell us on the car itself, but he was trying to get us to pay higher interest rates, purchase extended warranties, and probably pay $200 for floormats.

Some of the tactics he used included focusing on my wife, thinking she was less strong-willed than I was. That was a mistake. Then he did the *"let me go talk to my manager to see what we can do"* trick. He came back with the sales manager who asked what our concern was. We said we only wanted to pay so much and didn't want additional warranties. He asked, "If that's your only concern and I can address it, will you buy that car right here and now?" I recognized this as a persuasive trick to get us committed to something, a manipulation of our desires to appear consistent with ourselves.

The first sales guy took over again and went through this systematic process of trying to overcome our objections. It's a typical skill most sales people are trained on. I said something like, "Are you trying to overcome our objections now?" He didn't like that and, in the end, they wouldn't agree to our terms for buying that car. Having a little knowledge of persuasive techniques disarmed their strategies and we ended up leaving without buying the car. We got the same model from as different dealer. It was a waste of our time and theirs, but at least we felt good that we weren't manipulated into a purchase we'd later regret.

You can study these types of techniques in the book, *Influence: The Psychology of Persuasion* by Dr. Robert Cialdini. He identifies different tactics people use and he's put them into categories. For example, he talks about:

- The concept of **reciprocity**, when people give you something like a small gift or do a favor for you. Not because they like you or feel generous, but they expect to get something in exchange from you.

- Cialdini explains the concept of **consistency**, where people try to get you to make a commitment and sometimes expand the definition of what that commitment includes. This tactic of manipulating consistency often involves what we call bait-and-switch tactics. Bait-and-switch is defined as making promises or advertising goods that are an apparent bargain, with the intention of substituting inferior or more expensive goods, or failing to fulfill the promise made.

- Another strategy Dr. Cialdini has studied is leveraging the principle of **scarcity**. This is where people try to get you to take action by thinking if you don't, you'll miss out on an opportunity. Commercials say things like, "Act now before the price goes up!" Or, "For a Limited time only!" even though the store might have millions of them in their inventory and have no intention of raising the price. Don't let the fear of missing out (FOMO) override a rational decision.

I wrote the sales training programs for thousands of retail sales associates and telemarketers. I've created sales leadership and some management training programs that focus on employee compliance. I've become very familiar with some of the ways companies and their leadership try to persuade people. Let me mention a few more of those tactics. Again, I'm sharing this because simply knowing about them will strength your ability to resist them.

- One strategy salespeople and marketers use is the concept of a *perceived* discount. Do you know that retail price is a highly inflated cost for a product? Retail price is usually many times over what a company paid to get their products from a wholesaler. For example, if a dress has a retail price of $100, chances are that the company paid only 20-30 dollars for that item. If they put it on sale and say 20% off, you might go in and say, "Oh look at this, what a deal! It's 20% off. I'll save $20 if I buy it!" But not really. And if you do buy it, the company still made over $50 from you. Recognize the concept of perceived discounts and don't get pulled into a purchase based on that trick. Watch out for the *buy one get one free* tactics too.

- **Overcoming Objections**: Sales people and negotiators usually receive extensive training on a skill known as *overcoming objections*. They use it when they're trying to get you to agree to something they want you to do or to make a purchase. If you say, "No!", or something like "I need to think about it first," they have prepared responses for your objections. They have an arsenal of responses to use in each case. For example, they may try to make you afraid that you'll lose out on the opportunity of you don't agree to it now. They may even try to embarrass you, accusing you of being indecisive, cowardly, or abnormal if you don't agree to their proposal. It's easy to tell when someone launches into their overcoming objections phase of a sale, proposal, or negotiation. You can usually nullify these techniques by saying something like, "You don't need to try to overcome my objections. I'll decide for myself, thanks."

- **Selective Deafness**: Another technique manipulative people like to use is what's known as selective deafness. If you say no to what they're asking or if you ask a question the person doesn't want to give you the answer to, the manipulative person will act like he doesn't hear your refusal or your question. **They keep trying to persuade you and pretend you didn't already say no.** What's sad is that this trick often works on some people. They just get annoyed and become tired of resisting the person who's trying to persuade them and may finally give in. Don't let people persuade you with this cheap trick. Call them on it. Say, "You're *acting* like you didn't hear what I said. I said no. Do you think that pretending not to hear my answer is going to change my mind?"

- **The pull-back**: Another persuasive trick manipulative people use is known as the pull-back. It's where they suddenly stop putting pressure on you to do something. They attempt to make you afraid they're going to withdraw their offer, or change their mind, or refuse to work with you. They try to make you afraid of disappointing them and look like you wasted their time. But this is just another tactic to get you to do what they want. This is used a lot with children, and it's called reverse psychology. The adult form of reverse psychology, in one sense, is this pull-back strategy. Learn to recognize this trick and sidestep attempts to use it on you.

Most of these techniques are sales-focused. But watch out for these types of tricks in any industry, campaign, and in your relationships with other people.

Challenge: Your Experiences of Being Persuaded
Answer these questions:

- What types of persuasion have other people tried to use on you recently? How did it make you feel?

- What were the results of their persuasive attempts?

- Knowing what you know now about persuasion and manipulation, would you have reacted differently than you did? Why or why not?

- What do you plan to do to prevent persuasive attempts from influencing your thoughts and beliefs?

Bonus: How Einstein Got So Smart
This last section reinforces many of the concepts about learning better and improving your ability to think for yourself. It's a summary of an online course I created and I think it's a fitting end to this book.

How would you feel if many people thought you were the smartest person in history? How might your life be different if you were that intelligent? Although we often think of Albert Einstein as one of the smartest people ever, we don't investigate *how* he did it. People who speak highly of him often attribute his genius to some mysterious gift. They don't believe his smarts came from a unique attitude towards learning.

You can recreate his habits to improve your learning ability and find more rewarding work. Before you read the list of Einstein's learning habits, first consider some interesting facts about his early life. These things set the stage for appreciating his educational philosophy even more.

- Although he worked in engineering, Einstein's *father* failed at several business ventures and had to depend on relatives for support.

- When Einstein's father asked his son's headmaster what profession the boy should adopt, he said, "It doesn't matter; he'll never make a success of anything."

- He failed his first admissions examination to the Swiss scientific school he wanted to attend.

- Some family friends told Einstein's parents, "That young man will never amount to anything because he can't remember anything."

- After graduating from the university, officials denied Einstein a low-level teaching position there. Other friends in his graduating class did get teaching positions.

- Many scientists and professors stonewalled his requests to work for them.

- Einstein struggled for a few years to find employment and finally got work as a third-class government patent examiner.

- These things represent some of the irony about his early life. Looking back, considering his eventually-recognized genius, these facts seem humorous.

10 Things Einstein Did to Get So Smart

Here's the list of things (not everything) Einstein did to learn and to think independently. As you read through it, consider these questions: How can you apply these principles of learning to your own situation? How can adopting Einstein's habits help you improve your career or grow your business?

1. **He daydreamed and contemplated.** Who has the right to say what is absentmindedness and what's pure genius? What others labeled as forgetful or even spacey, Einstein knew to be some of his most insightful and creative brainstorming sessions.

2. **He rubbed shoulders with the best and brightest.** Especially after his reputation became known, Einstein sought out the instruction and mentorship of the smartest people in his field, like Max Planck. If he didn't get to know these people personally, he studied their writings and research.

3. **Einstein cross-trained.** He learned to play the violin well and loved the mathematical structure of music. He used music as a "psychological safety valve" throughout his life.

4. **He trusted his own curiosity.** One legendary story says that his father gave him a compass when he was five years old. After lengthy observation, Einstein figured out that some outside force acted on the needle to keep it pointed in the same direction.

5. **He maintained a deep suspicion of educational authority.** Too many teachers, even in our day, feel you should believe what they say because, "I said so." While they claim that thinking for yourself is part of the curriculum, their own biases discourage independent thought.

6. Einstein **nourished a *radical inquiring attitude*.** Remember the saying, "Those who ask a question are fools for five minutes; those who don't ask questions remain fools forever." True learning requires exploring assumptions and other facts that many take for granted.

7. Einstein **designed his own curriculum.** He had friends at the university take notes in class for him while he was away reading his preferred extracurricular books on physics and mathematics.

8. **He relied on faith to learn.** Einstein's faith was that by inquiry and discipline you could learn about invisible objects and phenomena. God is not arbitrary; He conforms to natural, discoverable laws.

9. **He avoided preoccupation with trivial things in life.** How much time would Einstein spend on *YouTube* or *Facebook* if he were around today? His mind consistently worked to explore and understand the physical world. What do you think about when you have nothing else to think about? Einstein's discoveries didn't come easily, they came from discipline!

10. **Einstein was an autodidact.** An autodidact is "a person who teaches himself or herself, rather than being taught by a teacher." (*Cambridge English Dictionary*) As biographer Ronald W. Clark wrote, he "found his real education elsewhere, in his own time." Schooling provided the basic building blocks of language and concepts, but Einstein's initiative took his learning far beyond the limits of academics.

Summary:

- Being flexible and versatile is the best way to get employment and income security.

- You need to learn to think for yourself. You should distrust what the masses believe and forge a path of your own ideas.

- You should assume nothing and work to develop your imagination.

- Reduce the influence social proof has on your thinking and decisions. The first step is to list all the social influences that adversely affect your life, and then identify ways to reduce their effect on you.

- Fear is a major enemy of thinking for yourself.

- Many people like reporters, politicians, and activists try to make you afraid so they can manipulate you.

- When you perceive a real or imagined threat, your brain functions differently; it retreats into survival mode and shuts down your rational thinking operations.

- A major step in learning to think more independently is to recognize when fear is hijacking your thought process. Simply recognizing this is the most important part of resisting it.

- You should be deeply suspicious of any organization or movement that relies primarily on fear to promote their agenda, including governments. People and organizations who use fear as their primary persuasive approach usually don't have valid reasons behind their causes or campaigns.

- When learning to resist persuasion, simply recognizing manipulative tricks helps to neutralize them.

- You can adopt Einstein's learning habits and philosophy to get wicked-smart.

19 WHAT'S NEXT?

This book on learning higher paying skills has given you some keys to open the doors of economic opportunity. However, what's included is just a small portion of things you can learn to get better work and income. The hope I have for this book is that it will **help you learn how to learn better**. If you've worked through this information and completed the challenges in each chapter, then you've demonstrated the necessary discipline to succeed in your professional pursuits.

Rather than tell you what to do next, I'm going to leave that responsibility with you. You determine what's next. Use your questioning, problem solving, researching, and decision-making skills to develop a plan for getting better work and income. Review the chapters in this book that you feel are most valuable. Please let me know what you think of this book; how it helped or how it can be improved. Use the contact link on *Didactable.com*.

Final Challenge: What's Next?

What steps are you going to take to get better work and income? How will you develop higher paying skills?

ABOUT THE AUTHOR

Steve Churchill is a learning strategist and instructional designer who's created hundreds of training programs for thousands of employees in many large companies, industries, and for organizational consulting firms. He's launched his own instructional media company, Didactable.com. He's committed to helping people get better work and income through learning higher paying skills. He earned Master's and Bachelor's degrees but his career and business depend on skills he learned primarily while on-the-job.

WHAT DO YOU THINK?

Please leave a review on the Amazon.com product page for this book. Let me and other potential readers know what you think. Just type in **"learn higher paying skills"** in the Amazon.com search box or use this link:

https://a.co/d/f9lFd6C

Scroll down to the bottom of the customer reviews and click the link, "Write a Customer Review." You need to log into your Amazon.com account to submit the review.

Made in United States
Troutdale, OR
04/08/2025

30457481R00120